# THE WORLD
# OF THE END

# THE WORLD
# OF THE END

## How Jesus' Prophecy
## Shapes Our Priorities

## DR. DAVID JEREMIAH

W PUBLISHING GROUP

AN IMPRINT OF THOMAS NELSON

Published in Nashville, Tennessee, by W Publishing, an imprint of Thomas Nelson.

Published in association with Yates & Yates, www.yates2.com.

Thomas Nelson titles may be purchased in bulk for educational, business, fundraising, or sales promotional use. For information, please email SpecialMarkets@ThomasNelson.com.

ISBN 978-0-7852-5199-6 (HC)
ISBN 978-0-7852-5211-5 (audiobook)
ISBN 978-0-7852-5210-8 (eBook)
ISBN 978-1-4003-3381-3 (IE)
ISBN 978-1-4041-1856-0 (custom)

**Library of Congress Control Number: 2022938395**

*Printed in the United States of America*

22 23 24 25 26  LSC  10 9 8 7 6 5 4 3 2 1

*To Rob Morgan*
*My faithful friend*

# Contents

# Introduction

Our world is in bad shape, and sometimes we feel that way too, don't we? In our better moments we know we're encompassed by God's blessing, yet we seem to struggle mightily with anxiety, fear, resentment, and discouragement. The chaos of the world seeps into our hearts. Fear can erode faith if we let it.

Is that true for you? At times, it sure is for me!

From long experience, I've learned that staying mentally healthy in a crumbling world is our daily assignment, and we can't do it without a buoyant spiritual foundation for our lives. We need God! We need Christ and His teachings. We need the Holy Spirit and His indwelling. And we need the Scripture and its prophecies about the future.

In these pages, I want to show you a special scene in the Bible in which the teachings of Christ, the inspiration of the Holy Spirit, and the prophetic words of God come together in a gripping chapter that's too often overlooked.

We call it the Olivet Discourse.

During the final week of His natural life, Jesus sat with four of His disciples on the ridge of the Mount of Olives. There at the crest of Olivet, our Lord rolled out the blueprint of the ages, the master plan for the last days.

Jesus began with a shocking prediction, one that seemed totally implausible in that moment. The massive temple complex, He said, would soon come tumbling down—every single stone! Then Jesus gazed further ahead into the World of the End, and He told us what would happen in the precarious days prior to His return.

In our days!

This is the greatest message on the future ever delivered, and it's recorded in Matthew 24 and 25, Mark 13, and Luke 21. (For this book, we will focus primarily on the opening verses of Matthew 24.)

Our Lord knows everything that has ever happened and that will ever happen. He knows it totally, in advance, and in detail; He understands the future into infinity. He already knows everything that will befall you during your lifetime, and He has offered powerful promises in His Word to reassure you of His presence and protection, and of His ordering of your days.

The future of the entire world is in His hands as well. Every sentence in Matthew 24 is addressed to you, if you're a child of God through Jesus Christ. They are for your information, anticipation, and motivation.

When we grasp the Message of Olivet, our plans and priorities will change. Our vision will shift from the immediate to the ultimate. We'll see today's headlines in the light of the hallelujahs of His return. We'll think better thoughts, feel healthier emotions, respond with better reactions, and do better things.

Christ's prophecy, then, must determine our priorities.

I've spent my adult life studying biblical prophecy, but I've never studied Matthew 24 more intensely than while preparing this book. To be honest, it seems I've had more spiritual opposition than usual while writing this book. The devil doesn't want us to know the Olivet Discourse. But Satan is already defeated, and his future condemnation is set.

The One who spoke the words on Olivet rules over the affairs of the nations, and He is relentlessly mobilizing the events of earth toward the imminent rapture of the church—the final battles of history, the splendor of His return, the unveiling of His kingdom, and the dazzling new heavens, new earth, and new city of Jerusalem.

We don't need to mope about our politics or global problems. We don't even have to settle for coping with the times. We have a hope as sure as the sunshine, as enduring as Scripture, and as glorious as the almighty throne of heaven.

In *The World of the End*, I want to show you how our priorities and lifestyles must align with these powerful words of Christ, which echo through history from that olive-covered ridge. For that reason, I've sought to make this book as practical as a toolbox.

In the first chapter I'll describe the dramatic setting and context in which Jesus spoke His prophecy. The following chapters will explain one event after another in our Lord's list of the signs of the times: deceivers will arise; wars and rumors of wars will escalate; disasters such as plagues, famines, and earthquakes will bedevil the world; and God's people will face increasing persecution, betrayal, lawlessness, and lovelessness. In spite of it all, the gospel will spread to the ends of the earth, and Christ will return right on schedule.

Those who keep going for Christ—who endure to the end—will be heroes in His sight.

That's why we must rededicate ourselves to our coming King in every area and activity of life. With His help, we can stay calm. We can remain confident and well prepared. We'll serve with uncommon faithfulness and unconditional love. As we hold up the cause of His cross, we'll be upheld by the power of His resurrection. As we take His gospel to the world, we will endure to the end.

The last part of every chapter in this book has a game plan of workable strategies for responding to the World of the End. We are not powerless. We may have limited control of what happens in our world, but we have extraordinary authority in Christ to determine how we react. We're not at the mercy of circumstances. We're empowered by the grace of God to leverage the events of life for Christ and His kingdom.

As Dr. David Osborn, professor emeritus of Christian leadership at Denver Seminary, says: "Too often we try to use God to change our circumstances, while he is using our circumstances to change us."[1]

You'll also find lots of stories and examples in the following pages. They're not there to entertain you. I've selected each one as an illustration for putting into daily practice the truths of biblical prophecy Jesus spelled out for us.

Never forget, prophecy is practical!

God lets us in on His plans for the future so we can establish our plans for today. His promises should shape our priorities and sustain our spirits. Billy Graham said, "When the 'evil day' comes, we do not have to be dependent upon the circumstances around us, but rather on the resources of God."[2]

Christians are not normal people. They are extraordinary people living with supernatural power in a downward-spiraling world. We are on a mission to help others and to spread gospel hope. There's a glorious work for you to do.

We can no longer operate with confusion or complacency. The last days are accelerating, and to me it's exhilarating. Let's stand as never before with biblical, Spirit-inspired determination, committed to serve Christ with all our hearts, whether by life or by death.

This I know with all my mind and believe with all my heart: time is short. Our Lord's words are unflagging and unfailing. They must shape our priorities and energize our plans. As we study our Lord's great sermon, every word of it underscores our mission. Every syllable establishes our glorious priorities as we await His impending return—that blessed hope—and as we say, *Amen! Even so, come Lord Jesus!*

# Chapter 1

# The Prophecy

*Jesus went out and departed from the temple, and His disciples came up to show Him the buildings of the temple. And Jesus said to them, "Do you not see all these things? Assuredly, I say to you, not one stone shall be left here upon another, that shall not be thrown down." Now as He sat on the Mount of Olives, the disciples came to Him privately, saying, "Tell us, when will these things be? And what will be the sign of Your coming, and of the end of the age?"*

MATTHEW 24:1–3

"And that's the way it is."

Sitting behind his desk at *CBS Evening News*, Walter Cronkite delivered that iconic sign-off for the final time on March 6, 1981. That moment put a wrap on an incredible journalistic career spanning forty-six years, three major wars—four if you count the Cold War—the civil rights movement, the assassinations of John F. Kennedy and Martin Luther King Jr., the Watergate scandal, and thousands of nightly broadcasts.

At the peak of his career, Cronkite spoke to twenty-nine million viewers every night. He shared the news of the day with honesty, impartiality, and a cool levelheadedness that helped his viewers remain calm even in the most uncertain of circumstances.

What is perhaps most remarkable about Walter Cronkite is that he understood the position he occupied within the culture, and he took it seriously. He often described his role as someone asked to "hold up the mirror—to tell and show the public what has happened." That was it. No flooding the airwaves with opinions. No strong-arming the public to move in this direction or that direction. He simply spoke the truth about the world, and in doing so he helped millions find their place in it.

Given that reality, perhaps it's not surprising that he was often identified as the most trusted man in America.[1]

Regrettably, there are no Walter Cronkites today—no voice or team of voices the majority of us trust to tell us what we need to know. Instead, our world is filled with innumerable prognosticators and prediction-makers ready to share their opinions. That includes approximately two million podcasters, six hundred thousand journalists, nearly four hundred twenty-four-hour news networks, and countless ministers all clamoring for your attention and all claiming accuracy and authority on what's happening today and what may happen tomorrow.

We hear so many voices. So many arguments. So many speculations. Everyone has a theory or an idea. Everyone is pushing some slant on the world—including what's in store for the future.

The clamor is louder than ever because we all have the feeling we're living in sudden-death overtime. Not until our own generation has technology provided so many potential ways for humanity to end. If you search online for "the end of the world," it's not sermons and preachers you'll find. It's scientists, statesmen, physicians, physicists, and secular sages.

In the midst of all this noise, I'd like to suggest there's one slant we should trust more than any other, one agenda we ought to prefer above all others, and one opinion we ought to value more than all the voices on earth. Amid the thousands of messages screaming for our attention, there's only one voice we need to hear.

The voice of the Lord Jesus Christ. He is the Mirror that can show us not just what is happening in the world but why it's happening—and what will happen next.

"But what does Jesus have to say about the future?" you ask.

A lot! It may surprise you to discover that one of the longest messages of Jesus recorded in the New Testament was all about the future.

Your future.

The Gospels of Matthew, Mark, and Luke all include a section often referred to as the Olivet Discourse (Matthew 24, Mark 13, Luke 21). That passage is so named because Jesus answered the questions of four of His disciples—Peter, James, John, and Andrew—while sitting on the Mount of Olives (Mark 13:3). Also known as Olivet, this area is a ridge east of Jerusalem that overlooks the city. It is a place Jesus often visited for rest and refuge.

Fewer than fifty days after His sermon on Olivet, Jesus ascended to heaven from that very mountain—perhaps from the very spot where He had preached. And to that same spot He will soon return to earth (Acts 1:12; Zechariah 14:4).

I've visited Olivet many times. Even today, it offers one of the most breathtaking views in the world, especially when the morning sun casts its glow across the golden city with its haunting walls, limestone buildings, ancient monuments, steeples, spires, and minarets. Dominating everything is the thirty-seven-acre powder keg known as al-Haram al-Sharif to Muslims and the Temple Mount to Jews and Christians. Whenever I visit, I instinctively think of our Lord's great sermon on the signs of the times and the end of the age.

Interestingly, many of the slopes of the Mount of Olives are now covered with concrete tombs. Faithful Jews want to be buried there so they'll be close at hand when the long-awaited Messiah arrives to enter the Eastern Gate of Jerusalem. No one knows how many people are buried there, but the number may reach 150,000, including the late Israeli prime minister Menachem Begin.

In our Lord's day, the hillsides were covered with olive trees, and the message Jesus gave His disciples on that historic day is—like the olive tree—ancient, sturdy, fruitful, and badly needed.

The Olivet Discourse is our Lord's second-longest recorded message in Matthew. The only one longer is the Sermon on the Mount (Matthew 5–7), which was a public sermon given at the beginning of Christ's earthly ministry. By contrast, the Olivet Discourse was a private message at the end of His earthly ministry.[2]

While the Olivet Discourse is the second-longest sermon of Jesus in Matthew, it ranks first in another category. It occupies more space than any other talk by Jesus in the entire Bible, when you consider it is recorded in Matthew, Mark, and Luke. It occupies two chapters in Matthew alone.

My friend and predecessor Dr. Tim LaHaye said this about Jesus' words: "The Olivet Discourse, delivered shortly before Jesus' crucifixion, is the most important single passage of prophecy in all the Bible. It is significant because it came from Jesus Himself immediately after He was rejected by His own people and because it provides the master outline of end-time events."[3]

## The Setting of the Prophecy

Matthew introduces us to Jesus' prophecy with these words: "Then Jesus went out and departed from the temple, and His disciples came up to show Him the buildings of the temple" (Matthew 24:1).

Let's enter the time machine of our imaginations and travel back to the time and place of Matthew 24. The Passover week would have fallen in early April, before the temperatures reached their oppressive summertime highs. Jesus and His disciples had trekked with crowds of pilgrims from Galilee, and everyone felt exuberant.

Everyone except, perhaps, Jesus, who had "set His face to go to Jerusalem" for this final trip (Luke 9:51).

Along the way He tried to prepare His disciples for the impending trauma of His arrest, trial, torture, death, and resurrection. But it was more than their minds could absorb. Who can blame them? A crucified Messiah wasn't part of their worldview. Instead, they expected to soon sit at His right and left hand as He fulfilled the Old Testament promises of the coming kingdom (Matthew 20:21).

The Lord and His companions walked through the Jordan Valley to Jericho, where He healed two blind beggars and gave them sight (Matthew 20:29–34). Then they ascended the old Jericho Road, hiking upward toward the backside of the Mount of Olives. When they arrived in Bethany, Jesus visited with friends who lived there. Mary and Martha prepared supper, and Lazarus undoubtedly again thanked Jesus for restoring his life. Mary anointed His feet with oil, and the house was filled with that fragrance (John 12:1–7).

Our Lord had less than a week to live.

When the Galilean guests woke on Sunday morning, they trudged up the eastern side of Olivet to the crest, and then Jesus asked His disciples to fetch Him a colt. In stark contrast to the Jerusalem crowd that would reject Him in just a few days, large crowds of Galilean pilgrims welcomed Him by singing, "Hosanna to the Son of David! 'Blessed is He who comes in the name of the LORD!' Hosanna in the highest!" (Matthew 21:9). Jesus entered the temple briefly before returning to Bethany for the night.

On Monday morning, Jesus cursed a fruitless fig tree on His way back into the Holy City (Mark 11:12–14). Later that day, He caused a stir in the temple as He overturned the tables of the money changers (Mark 11:15–18). The chief priests and scribes were angry enough to kill Him. Monday evening, He returned to Bethany with the twelve disciples for the night.

That brings us to the day of Jesus' great prophecy. On Tuesday morning, Jesus returned to the temple. There He delivered a blistering rebuke to the Jewish leaders and the nation of Israel. Have you ever been in a public place when a violent argument broke out— the kind in which conversations cease and everyone's attention is glued to the conflict? Today people would pull out their cellphones to record the scene. Matthew didn't have a cell phone, but you can't read his account without picturing it in your mind and feeling the tension.

Jesus' blistering words are recorded in Matthew 21-23. The same Lord who began His teaching ministry with a series of beatitudes ("Blessed are . . .") in Matthew 5 concluded His public ministry with a series of curses ("Woe to you . . .") in Matthew 23.

Bible commentator Dr. John Walvoord wrote:

As Christ dealt with spiritual, theological, and moral apostasy in His day in Matthew 23, He delivered the most scathing denunciation of false religion and hypocrisy to be found anywhere. He calls the scribes and the Pharisees hypocrites no less than seven times (Matt 23:13, 14, 15, 23, 25, 27, 29). He calls them blind five times (Matt 23:16, 17, 19, 24, 26), labels them fools twice (Matt 23:17, 19), describes them as whited sepulchers (Matt 23:27), serpents or snakes, the children of poisonous vipers (Matt 23:33), and declares that they are in danger of going to hell. It would be difficult to find words more biting than these words of Christ used to characterize the religion of His day.[4]

Jesus spoke with righteous anger, and His fiery words condemned the Jewish leaders and their nation for rejecting Him. At the same time, His heart was breaking. These were His people! He loved them and the city of Jerusalem. Looking out over the houses, streets, and buildings covering the hills and deep ravines of that ancient Jewish capital, He wept, saying:

> O Jerusalem, Jerusalem, the one who kills the prophets and stones those who are sent to her! How often I wanted to gather your children together, as a hen gathers her chicks under her wings, but you were not willing! See! Your house is left to you desolate; for I say to you, you shall see Me no more till you say, "Blessed is He who comes in the name of the LORD!" (Matthew 23:37–39)

The last thing Jesus did before He left the temple on Tuesday evening was to sit opposite the temple treasury and watch people give their tithes and offerings. He watched as the rich gave much but a poor widow only her two mites (Mark 12:41 44).

Tuesday drew to a close. Only three days left. With perhaps a poignant backward glance, Jesus departed the temple, symbolizing the withdrawal of God's presence from that sacred place (Matthew 24:1). He sadly descended the staircase, leaving the mount where His people should have received Him. They would see Him no more until they were ready to say, "Blessed is He who comes in the name of the LORD!" (Matthew 23:39).

That's when the disciples remarked to Jesus, "Teacher, look at these magnificent buildings! Look at the impressive stones in the walls" (Mark 13:1 NLT).

There's a lot of conjecture about why the disciples chose that moment to become infatuated with the temple buildings. I confess I'm not sure about the cause. Perhaps it was because the barrenness of their inward lives had been exposed. In other words, their spiritual lives might have been empty, but they sure were proud of the beautiful buildings they had built.

Perhaps the disciples wanted to distract Jesus and themselves from the emotional exhaustion they had gone through. Perhaps the sun, low in the sky, sent cascades of gold across the stones and through the columns, and they were simply awestruck by the beauty of what they saw.

We might not know exactly what the disciples were thinking about the temple that Tuesday evening, but it's pretty clear what Jesus thought about it. It is remarkable that Jesus spent the entire last week leading up to the cross focused on the temple and the corruption taking place there. The temple had become a place of financial greed where false religion and hypocrisy abounded and where poor widows were being robbed. God's people had made a mockery of the temple and its very purpose—and for that, judgment was coming soon. Jesus had had enough.

## The Subject of the Prophecy

Jesus responded to the disciples' awe of the temple buildings by sitting down with them on the Mount of Olives (Matthew 24:2-3). In that culture, sitting was the posture of a teacher giving an important lesson. This is the final extended sermon in the gospel of Matthew, and it's Jesus' most important lesson about the end of history. You can read the entire message in Matthew 24 and 25.

From their vantage on the Mount of Olives, Jesus and His disciples had a staggering view of Jerusalem and the temple complex. It was there, at that place and moment, that Jesus made a stunning prediction about the future.

## The Profound Prediction

In Matthew 24:2, Jesus said, "Do you not see all these things? Assuredly, I say to you, not one stone shall be left here upon another, that shall not be thrown down."

What was Jesus doing when He predicted the utter destruction of the temple in Jerusalem? We dare not miss the significance of this!

His words were breathtaking and definitive because He intended to show us His infallibility as a prophet. He said something so profound it could hardly be believed, yet so historic it could not later be denied. He was giving a specific prediction that would be fulfilled to the exact letter, as no historian can now dispute. He foresaw the soon-coming total destruction of everything they were gazing at—the entire series of edifices on the Temple Mount.

This wasn't the first time Jesus had predicted the destruction of the temple. When He rebuked the Jews for their unbelief a chapter earlier, Jesus told them, "Your house is left to you desolate" (Matthew 23:38).

Jesus was also speaking about the city of Jerusalem, and particularly the temple, when He said this on the day of His triumphal entry:

> If you had known, even you, especially in this your day, the things that make for your peace! But now they are hidden from your eyes. For days will come upon you when your enemies will build an embankment around you, surround you and close you in on every side, and level you, and your children within you, to the ground; and they will not leave in you one stone upon another, because you did not know the time of your visitation. (Luke 19:42–44)

The temple complex Jesus gestured to across the Kidron Valley was built on the same spot as Solomon's great temple, which is described in the Old Testament. That building had been destroyed by the armies of Babylon in 586 BC and later replaced by a smaller temple, which is described in the book of Ezra.

# THE TEMPLE: GOD'S DWELLING PLACE

**The Mosaic Tabernacle (1445 BC)**
Exodus 25–31, 40

**Solomon's Temple (966–586 BC)**
2 Chronicles 2–3

**Zerubbabel's Temple (520 BC)**
Ezra 6

**Herod's Temple (20 BC–AD 70)**
Luke 21:5; John 2:20; Mark 13:1

**The Tribulation Temple**
Daniel 9:27;
Matthew 24:15–16;
2 Thessalonians 2:3–4

**The Millennial Temple**
Ezekiel 40–48

**The Eternal Temple**
Revelation 21:22

Herod the Great started renovating this smaller temple before Jesus' birth. Actually, it was more than a renovation. Herod created one of the wonders of the ancient world. The reconstruction process had been going on for more than forty years by that point and wasn't actually completed until AD 64. Jesus was gazing across the valley at a magnificent structure built of stones weighing many tons, some of them twenty feet long and twelve feet high. They were carved from quarries underneath and around the city of Jerusalem, and they were cut precisely to size. With great labor, using rollers and earth inclines to raise them to their proper height, those stones were fitted into the buildings of the temple without the need for mortar.

Herod sought to rival Solomon in order to fulfill Haggai's prediction that the latter temple would be greater than the former (Haggai 2:9). He employed ten thousand skilled workmen along with a thousand priests, all acquainted with fine work in wood and stone. Herod doubled the original area of the Temple Mount by constructing huge supporting walls and leveling the terrain. This renewed temple complex became a source of pride for Jews the world over.[5]

The historian Josephus described the temple complex as "the most admirable of all the works that we have seen or heard of, both for its curious structure and its magnitude, and also for the vast wealth bestowed upon it, as well as for the glorious reputation it had for its holiness."[6]

The rabbis said: "He who has not seen the temple in its full splendor has never seen a beautiful building."[7]

The temple was one of the most expansive, majestic, and important buildings in the world.

But not for long. In a few terse words, Jesus made a profound prediction—one that must have stunned the four disciples who heard it and the three disciples who recorded it for us in their gospels.

## The Precise Performance

While Luke 19 provides us with a description of the destruction of Jerusalem, the first-century historian Josephus also gave us a detailed record of how Jesus' temple prophecy came to pass. It was fulfilled down to the last letter and literally down to the last stone.[8]

Fast-forward to AD 70. Responding to a Jewish insurgency throughout Judea, the Roman general Titus built large wooden scaffolds around the walls of the temple buildings—a tactic never before used. He piled the scaffolds high with wood and other flammable items and set them on fire. The intense heat weakened the temple structure, and the Romans were able to dislodge the giant stones, prying them off one by one and casting them into the valley below. Afterward, soldiers sifted through the rubble left on the temple site to retrieve any gold that had melted into the smoldering ruins. All that remained on the site was flattened down to the retaining walls—just as Jesus had predicted.[9]

What are the odds that Jesus could accurately "guess" about a huge and hugely honored temple being destroyed within a few decades? What is the likelihood that His "guess" could be accurate to the very stones on the ground? The statistical probability boggles the mind. But when Jesus speaks, odds mean nothing. What He predicts comes true. What He prophesies happens—precisely as He says it will.

And so, less than forty years after our Lord's message, the temple was gone. Today the location is a walled compound within the Old City of Jerusalem. In the southwest stands the Western Wall—the retaining wall of Herod's Temple Mount. Visitors to the southern steps of the Temple Mount can still see some of the massive stones scattered like giant building blocks.

Why am I dwelling on that historical moment? Because one of the keys to understanding Jesus' words about the world at the end of history is to understand that His prophecies were fulfilled exactly as He said they would be. They are precise. And nothing illustrates that truth more powerfully than Jesus' prophecy concerning the destruction of Herod's temple.

That prophecy is the prelude to the Olivet Discourse, and it allows us to verify the accuracy of the words Jesus spoke that day. Because His words—improbable as they seemed at the time—came exactly true in history now past, we can fully depend on the accuracy of the rest of what He said about the future. We can have every confidence in their precise fulfillment.

Perhaps sparked by Jesus' blunt promises, the disciples responded by asking Him two questions: "Tell us, when will these things be? And what will be the sign of Your coming, and of the end of the age?" (Matthew 24:3).

In Matthew 24:4–8, Jesus began to answer by describing the initial group of what we often call "the signs of the times"—the things that will happen just before He returns. We'll devote the rest of this book to studying this revelation in detail:

Take heed that no one deceives you. For many will come in My name, saying, "I am the Christ," and will deceive many. And you will hear of wars and rumors of wars. See that you are not troubled; for all these things must come to pass, but the end is not yet. For nation will rise against nation, and kingdom against kingdom. And there will be famines, pestilences, and earthquakes in various places. All these are the beginning of sorrows.

## The Secret to the Prophecy

The secret to understanding our Lord's prophecy is found in that final word, which is translated "sorrows" in the New King James Version. The Greek term used in Matthew 24:8 is *odin*, which literally means birth pains—the contractions that begin and increase during the birth of a baby.

Those contractions occur when the muscles of a woman's uterus tighten and release, which prepares her body to give birth. At first, these contractions may be rather mild and irregular. But as the delivery draws closer, the contractions become stronger, closer together, more regular, and more painful. When the contractions are coming quickly and intensely, you'd better get to the hospital or you'll be giving birth in the back seat of the car.

The apostle Paul used the same figure of speech when he discussed the return of Christ with the believers in Thessalonica, saying, "But concerning the times and the seasons, brethren, you have no need that I should write to you. For you yourselves know perfectly that the day of the Lord so comes as a thief in the night. For when they say, 'Peace and safety!' then sudden destruction comes upon them, as labor pains upon a pregnant woman. And they shall not escape" (1 Thessalonians 5:1–3).

The epoch Jesus described in Matthew 24 is also pictured in the book of Revelation where "the seal judgments unfold over a period of perhaps years (6:1–8:1–6), the trumpet judgments over a much shorter period of time, perhaps weeks (see 8:7–9:21; 11:15–19), and the bowl judgments over the period of perhaps a few days or even hours (Revelation 16:1–21)."[10]

# The Birth Pains Principle in the Book of Revelation

**YEARS**

## 7 SEALS

1. White Horse—*The Conquering Power*
2. Red Horse—*War and Bloodshed*
3. Black Horse—*Famine*
4. Pale Horse—*Pestilence and Death*
5. Souls Under the Altar—*Martyrs*
6. Whole World Trembles—*Physical Changes*
7. Silence—*The Golden Censer*

Revelation 6:1-17; 8:1-5

**WEEKS**

## 7 TRUMPETS

1. Hail and Fire Mixed With Blood
2. Mountain Thrown Into the Sea
3. The Star Wormwood
4. A Third of the Sun, Moon, & Stars Struck
5. The Plague of Locusts
6. Release of the Four Angels
7. Woe on Earth, Worship in Heaven

Revelation 8:6-9:21; 11:15-19

**DAYS *or* HOURS**

## 7 BOWLS

1. Ugly and Painful Sores
2. Sea Turns to Blood
3. Rivers & Streams of Water Become Blood
4. Sun Scorches People With Fire
5. Darkness
6. Euphrates River Dries Up
7. Tremendous Earthquake—Armageddon

Revelation 16:1-21

What Jesus wants us to know as we unpack the rest of His sermon is this: the things that are going to happen in the future will not be all-of-a-sudden experiences. They will be like birth pains, with the frequency and intensity of each event gradually increasing. When we observe that pattern in the world, we've discovered the secret to understanding the signs of the times.

## The Scope of the Prophecy

Wilbur Smith, a prominent scholar of the previous generation, called the Olivet Discourse the most neglected discourse of Jesus Christ. I think he was correct, and I think I know why.

Some who have written about this subject have buried this message of Jesus in history. In other words, they want us to believe everything Jesus said to His disciples was fulfilled in AD 70 when Titus destroyed Jerusalem. Several of these writers have even tried to convince us the second coming of Christ happened in AD 70.

Others believe that Jesus' words have nothing to do with today's world. They take a two-pronged approach: (1) What Jesus said about the temple being destroyed has already happened, and (2) the remainder of the Lord's prophecy won't be triggered until the church is removed during the rapture. This was actually my view when I was a student in seminary.

But over the years I've come to believe these words of Jesus are for us today. They are for me, and they are for you.

Perhaps I wasn't listening as carefully as I should have been in seminary, because the president of that school at the time was John Walvoord, one of our most respected prophecy scholars. Here's what he wrote about the Olivet Discourse—and this aligns with my own convictions today:

> The words of Christ to His disciples on the Mount of Olives delivered not long before He died have dramatic contemporary significance. In this discourse, Christ answered their questions concerning the signs of the end of the age and of His second coming. The revelation becomes increasingly vital to understanding the meaning of events that are occurring today. . . . A study of these prophecies will help one to understand the headlines of our newspapers today.[11]

In his book *Prophecy Made Plain*, Carl G. Johnson wrote, "As I have studied this chapter, I am convinced that we have in the first eight verses a picture of this present age."[12]

In other words, the signs Jesus promised are like birth pains. They are occurring now, increasing in frequency, and pointing toward the rapture of the church. But the moment the church is gone, those signs will become much more severe and will throw the post-rapture world of the tribulation into a state of seizures and spasms such as we see described in the book of Revelation. In fact, the signs of Matthew 24 line up perfectly with the seals of Revelation 6. It is uncanny how accurate the Word of God really is.

# MATTHEW 24 & REVELATION 6

| THE SIGNS OF THE OLIVET DISCOURSE | THE SEAL JUDGMENTS OF REVELATION |
|---|---|
| False Christs and False Prophets (Matthew 24:4–5, 11) | White Horse: Antichrist (Revelation 6:2) |
| Wars and Rumors of Wars (Matthew 24:6–7) | Red Horse: War and Bloodshed (Revelation 6:3–4) |
| Famines (Matthew 24:7) | Black Horse: Famine (Revelation 6:5–6) |
| Pestilence and Death (Matthew 24:7–8) | Pale Horse: Pestilence and Death (Revelation 6:7–8) |

None of that means we're exempt from the buildup of these birth pains today. Jesus' prophecy applies to us at this critical hour of history. While it does not tell us when the rapture will occur, it does describe what life will be like during the season of the rapture. Yes, after the rapture these signs will be solidified and fully realized during the first half of the tribulation. Yet they will not appear out of nowhere. They will represent the continuation and intensification of what was already unfolding on the world stage.

When Christ comes in the air for His church (1 Thessalonians 4:17), every single Christian on earth will be removed—and with the Christians, the indwelling Holy Spirit, who is the restrainer of all evil. At that point, all hell will break loose, and the signs given in Matthew 24:4–14 will accelerate to tribulation speed.

Here's my point: we may not be living at the end of the world, but we are living in the World of the End!

# The Significance of the Prophecy

As I mentioned earlier, what Jesus shared in His Olivet Discourse is not some ivory-tower speech with no impact on our lives. He spoke each word carefully and precisely, and each one is meant to help you and me on a personal level. They are just as relevant to us as His first sermon in Matthew—the Sermon on the Mount.

I never want to impart biblical information without making sure we see the spiritual lessons in every page and every verse. As I pored over these first three verses (Matthew 24:1–3), three things struck me about our current life—the day-to-day activities and attitudes lived out by followers of Christ.

## Jesus Wants to Teach Us About the Future

First, Jesus wants us to study the future. Our Lord was in the habit of preparing His disciples for upcoming events even during His days on this earth. As we've seen, He made a point of telling those around Him some of the things they could anticipate in the days ahead. So don't let anyone tell you Jesus didn't bother about the future or was uninterested in prophecy. The facts speak otherwise.

Not to mention Scripture says otherwise. "J. Barton Payne's *Encyclopedia of Biblical Prophecy* lists 1,239 prophecies in the Old Testament and 578 prophecies in the New Testament for a total of 1,817. These encompass 8,352 verses out of 31,102"—or more than a quarter of God's Word![13]

If the future was an important subject to Jesus and the biblical writers, it should be important to us as well. It should be something we are always studying and learning about.

Theologian Wayne Grudem wrote, "Although we cannot know everything about the future, God knows everything about the future and he has in Scripture told us about the major events yet to come in the history of the universe. About these events occurring we can have absolute confidence because God is never wrong and never lies."[14]

The Olivet Discourse was one of the ways Jesus warned His disciples, including you and me, about the end of history. He showed us the signs to watch for and how to live. The question is: Will we listen? Will we respond?

If we do listen, we won't be surprised by the future. We will recognize the signs of the times, and we will properly handle the strains of everyday life as we anticipate His return and strive to live for Him even in the World of the End.

## Jesus Wants to Transform Us for the Future

Second, Christ's prophetic ministry also transforms us so we'll be able to meet the demands of the future. Jesus said, "These things I have spoken to you [about the future], that you should not be made to stumble" (John 16:1). A few verses later, He added, "These things I have told you, that when the time comes, you may remember that I told you of them" (v. 4).

In other words, "If you grasp what I am telling you about the future, you won't fall all over yourself. You won't fall into the trap of running around in panic mode when you can trust Me instead. You won't be blown off course because you will have a sense of what God is up to."

If you are looking for a manual to the future that places no demands upon you today or a guidebook for days to come that has no bearing on days right now, you've come to the wrong place. I can't get excited about any book that inspires concern about future events but ignores what God wants us to do today. My study of prophecy convinces me that God intends knowledge of future events to help us occupy our world with a sense of urgency until the Lord returns.

Paul Benware wrote, "A believer who gets out of bed in the

morning thinking *My Lord Jesus could return today* will probably not let sin take root in his life. But Christians who rarely, if ever, reflect on the realities of the future life, the Lord's coming, and the judgment seat of Christ are far more vulnerable to temptation and sin. And perhaps that explains something of the sin and apathy seen in much of the church today."[15]

## Jesus Wants Us to Trust Him with the Future

Finally, as human beings, we often get things wrong when we try to predict the future. For example, during a 2007 interview with *USA Today*, Microsoft CEO Steve Ballmer opined, "There's no chance that the iPhone is going to get any significant market share. No chance." Ballmer based this prediction on the notion that iPhones would be interesting to technology nerds, but not to the general population. "I want to have products that appeal to everybody," he said.[16]

Fifteen years later, with more than two billion iPhones sold, it's safe to say Steve Ballmer was wrong.

What about Jesus, then? Why exactly can you and I be sure that His prophecies will come true? Why can we trust that He is telling us the truth about the future?

In the prologue to the book of Revelation, the apostle John answered those questions by giving us one of the most profound reasons imaginable for listening to the prophetic words of Christ. John was on the Isle of Patmos when he saw the One to whom we should listen, and this is how he described the encounter: "When I saw Him, I fell at His feet as dead. But He laid His right hand on me, saying to me, 'Do not be afraid; I am the First and the Last. I am He who lives, and was dead, and behold, I am alive forevermore. Amen. And I have the keys of Hades and of Death. Write the things which you have seen, and the things which are, and the things which will take place after this'" (Revelation 1:17–19).

Who else do you know who has one foot planted in eternity and the other planted in time? Who do you know who actually lives in the present and in the future and says to us today, "This is what you should expect as you await My return"?

No one ever grasped the future as firmly and completely as the Lord Jesus Christ. He sees it all, and He knows it all. As the eternal God, He sees the whole parade of humanity from beginning to end, from Adam to Antichrist. We see little snatches of it, but Jesus alone is the Alpha and Omega.

"I am God, and there is no other; I am God, and there is none like Me, declaring the end from the beginning, and from ancient times things that are not yet done, saying, 'My counsel shall stand, and I will do all My pleasure'. . . . Indeed I have spoken it; I will also bring it to pass. I have purposed it; I will also do it" (Isaiah 46:9–11).

The lesson is clear: you can trust our Lord and Savior with the future! And not just with "the future" generally, but with *your* future specifically.

Now we can understand why Jesus didn't answer the disciples' two questions in great detail. In fact, He didn't even answer one of their questions—the question about the timing of the destruction of the temple. Instead, He gave them a series of signs of what the World of the End would look like. Jesus was reminding His disciples that they didn't have to figure out how all the pieces of the end-times puzzle would fit together. Instead, their responsibility was to trust Him with the future and remain faithful to Him until the end.

When pastor Mark Mitchell began studying the Olivet Discourse, he thought of his own experience training for a marathon. The most uncertain part of the course for him involved the final six miles. A marathon covers more than twenty-six miles, but Mark's training regime stopped at twenty. As he trained month after month, he never ran more than twenty miles at a time.

He wondered what those final miles would be like. They were a no-man's-land to him, and he wondered if he would give out, suffer cramps, or be able press on to the finish line. Ultimately, he believed his training would propel him the rest of the way, so he paced himself and persevered to the end.

He later wrote,

> We read a passage like [Matthew 24], and it's like we're reading about the last six miles of a marathon. We know it's going to be hard, and we know that there is nothing we can do now to replicate what it will be like then. But Jesus has told us what to look for and how to be prepared—how to cross the finish line.
>
> We prepare by being wise and discerning about the false claims of religious hucksters. We prepare by resting in the fact that God is sovereign and whatever happens to us is part of his plan. We prepare by trusting that he's creating opportunities for us to bear witness, and he'll give us the words we need when we need them. We prepare by learning to endure hardship so that when greater hardship comes, we don't fall by the wayside. We prepare by refusing to allow ourselves to buy the lie that the things of this world are the most important things. We prepare by praying each day for God's strength to face whatever the last six miles of life may hold for us.[17]

That's the focus of the rest of this book. Jesus gave us this prophecy to prepare us for what's to come—for the last six miles of the world—and I want to share His advice with you. He didn't give us this information so we would be afraid of what's to come or be overwhelmed by the World of the End. He knows what's ahead, and He wants to make sure we can face it with confidence and hope. He wants us to be "blameless and harmless, children of God without fault in the midst of a crooked and perverse generation, among whom you shine as lights in the world, holding fast the word of life" (Philippians 2:15–16).

Jesus has told us about the final six miles of the race, so let's make up our minds to run with perseverance, looking ever unto Him, the author and finisher of our faith (Hebrews 12:1–2).

Chapter 2

# IN A WORLD OF DECEPTION,
# *BE HONEST*

*Jesus answered and said to them: "Take heed*
*that no one deceives you. For many will*
*come in My name, saying, 'I am the Christ,'*
*and will deceive many. . . . Then many false*
*prophets will rise up and deceive many."*
MATTHEW 24:4–5, 11

The end came swiftly—4:00 p.m. local time on Christmas Day, 1989. Nicolae Ceauşescu and his wife, Elena, hands bound, faces defiant, faced a firing squad of Romanian paratroopers. In a blazing instant, their bodies absorbed 120 rounds of ammunition, and one of the twentieth century's most brutal reigns came to an end. Those executions also signaled the end of the collection of Communist regimes known as the Soviet Bloc.

Ceaușescu was a master of deception. His striking face could be stern, happy, terrifying—whatever he wanted it to be. He and his wife kept an iron grip on Romania for twenty-four years, promising to turn the nation into a utopia, a country without oppression or poverty, a place of plenty and prosperity.

All the while, their cruel fists were crushing their own people and squeezing their nation dry.

Ceaușescu presented himself as a man of unprecedented talent: "the supreme embodiment of good," the "Hero of Heroes," the "Worker of Workers," and the "First Personage of the World."[1]

His wife, Elena, was an attractive woman from a peasant background who was determined to be as powerful as her husband. She became first deputy prime minister and the "Mother of the Nation." The media hailed her as a model for women everywhere.

If so, she was a model like Jezebel. In fact, their story bears striking resemblance to King Ahab and Queen Jezebel of Old Testament infamy. It's the story of an arrogant couple who were addicted to power and reigned through deceit, duplicity, and unimaginable cruelty—with a disastrous ending.

Many historians will tell you the Ceaușescus were as evil as Hitler; they simply lacked the opportunity to work on as grand a scale. They deceived not only their own people but also the West. Queen Elizabeth II knighted Ceaușescu. The United States government granted his country "most-favored nation" trading status. Former Israeli prime minister Menachem Begin credited Ceaușescu with mediating Anwar Sadat's peace mission to Jerusalem.

This couple fooled the world for decades.

Unfortunately, they aren't the last of the great deceivers. Counterfeit leaders are still proliferating like spores in the air, growing worse by the day. This trend won't end until the Antichrist meets his doom.

Deception is a frequent topic in Scripture. It begins in the garden of Eden when Eve said, "The serpent deceived me, and I ate" (Genesis 3:13). At the other end of the Bible, we read something similar: "The devil, who deceived them, was cast into the lake of fire" (Revelation 20:10).

Think of it: the master deceiver—Satan—enters the picture three chapters into the Bible, and he is cast into the lake of fire three chapters from the end of the Bible. From Eden to the end, he's been spinning webs of deception and smothering our world.

Jesus took keen notice of this theme in His Olivet Discourse. Deceit occupies a significant place in the prophetic passages of the New Testament, and this is actually where Jesus began His teaching about signs of the times. When the disciples came to Jesus and asked Him about the future, He began His response by saying, "Take heed that no one deceives you" (Matthew 24:4).

## The Status of Deception in the World of the End

According to Jesus, disinformation will play a major role in the World of the End. While we should always be on the alert for lies and misdirection, the Lord warned us to be especially watchful for spiritual deceit as the day of His return approaches:

- "Jesus, answering them, began to say: 'Take heed that no one deceives you. For many will come in My name, saying, "I am He," and will deceive many'" (Mark 13:5–6).
- "He said: 'Take heed that you not be deceived. For many will come in My name, saying, "I am He," and, "The time has drawn near." Therefore do not go after them'" (Luke 21:8).

- "Then if anyone says to you, 'Look, here is the Christ!' or 'There!' do not believe it. For false christs and false prophets will rise and show great signs and wonders to deceive, if possible, even the elect" (Matthew 24:23–24).

As I've mentioned, the judgments promised in Matthew 24:4–11 parallel the first five seal judgments of Revelation 6:1–11. The first seal depicts a false messiah:

Now I saw when the Lamb opened one of the seals; and I heard one of the four living creatures saying with a voice like thunder, "Come and see." And I looked, and behold, a white horse. He who sat on it had a bow; and a crown was given to him, and he went out conquering and to conquer. (Revelation 6:1–2)

This rider on the white horse is a counterfeit. He is a false christ. He will arise as a global champion, the person of the hour, to rescue the world from impending catastrophe. In short order, he will mutate into the Antichrist. But this personage won't simply appear in a vacuum. Leading up to his appearance, many others will come and falsely claim to be the Messiah (1 John 2:18). Our Lord specifically instructed His disciples not to fall for such claims.

Is the idea far-fetched? People claiming messiahship? Figures claiming to be the Savior? No! Even in the first century, several revolutionaries made that boast and are mentioned in the book of Acts.

First was Theudas. Luke wrote, "For some time ago Theudas rose up, claiming to be somebody. A number of men, about four hundred, joined him. He was slain, and all who obeyed him were scattered and came to nothing" (Acts 5:36).

The first-century historian Josephus tells the story of Theudas, who promised freedom to his followers:

> Now it came to pass, while Fadus was procurator of Judea, that a certain magician, whose name was Theudas, persuaded a great part of the people to take their effects with them, and follow him to the river Jordan; for he told them he was a prophet, and that he would, by his own command, divide the river, and afford them an easy passage over it; and many were deluded by his words.
>
> However, Fadus did not permit them to make any advantage of his wild attempt, but sent a troop of horsemen out against them; who, falling upon them unexpectedly, slew many of them, and took many of them alive. They also took Theudas alive, and cut off his head, and carried it to Jerusalem.[2]

Another deceiver was known only as "the Egyptian" in the New Testament: "Are you not the Egyptian who some time ago stirred up a rebellion and led the four thousand assassins out into the wilderness?" (Acts 21:38).

Josephus also describes this Egyptian who came to Jerusalem claiming to be a prophet:

> There came out of Egypt about this time to Jerusalem one that said he was a prophet, and advised the multitude of the common people to go along with him to the Mount of Olives, as it was called, which lay over against the city, and at the distance of five furlongs. He said further, that he would show them from hence how, at his command, the walls of Jerusalem would fall down; and he promised them that he would procure them an entrance into the city through those walls, when they were fallen down.

Now when Felix was informed of these things, he ordered his soldiers to take their weapons, and came against them with a great number of horsemen and footmen from Jerusalem, and attacked the Egyptian and the people that were with him. He also slew four hundred of them, and took two hundred alive. But the Egyptian himself escaped out of the fight, but did not appear any more.[3]

About a hundred years after Christ, another false savior named Bar Kokhbah appeared in Judea. Jerusalem had been defeated by Rome, and Bar Kokhbah took upon himself the aura of the long-awaited Messiah. He was a remarkable figure, but his rebellion ended in tragedy.

The revolt was extinguished by the Roman emperor Hadrian around AD 135. "Roman soldiers, with extra legions sent from abroad, spent four years suppressing the revolt. The war was devastating. The legions destroyed 50 fortresses, 985 settlements, and killed 580,000 fighters and innumerable others who died of starvation and illness."[4]

In every century after Christ's death and resurrection, impostors have claimed to be the Messiah or some other sort of savior to their people or to the world. Without fail, they have all been pretenders.

But it's not only false messiahs that are the problem. For every impostor who has claimed to be the Messiah, at least ten others claim knowledge they don't have about a future they cannot know. They are false prophets. Jesus warned us about these individuals as well: "Then many false prophets will rise up and deceive many" (Matthew 24:11).

In the 1800s, a New Englander named William Miller became enamored with determining the date of the imminent return of Christ, using dubious mathematical calculations. He collected mounds of data, analyzed it, and was certain Christ would return on March 21, 1843.

The press went wild, and the news spread across the country. As March 21 approached, businesses ceased, people stayed home, and Miller's devoted followers donned their ascension robes, trekked into the mountains, and climbed towering trees to get as high as possible so they would have "less distance to travel through the air" when the Lord returned with a shout.

The day came and went. The Lord didn't return. The Millerites trudged home, accompanied by jeers and catcalls from their neighbors and friends. It was a confusing day for these disappointed men and women. Even worse, it made everyone who followed the news a bit more cynical about Christianity.

William Miller wasn't a man to give up easily. He went back to the Scriptures and found a one-year "mistake" in his calculations. Exactly 365 days later, the Millerites once again robed themselves, climbed trees, and awaited the Lord's return. And once again, they were disappointed and angry. Most of them turned their hearts away from their sincere but deluded leader—and infinitely more tragic, some turned their hearts away from God.

To his credit, Miller himself repented of his date setting and publicly admitted he had made a terrible error, not merely in his calculations but in his foolish attempts to set the date of Christ's return. By then, of course, the damage was done.[5]

Miller is not alone. Many other people have speculated on the day and hour of the Lord's return, some of them making specific predictions about the end of the world. Frankly, when I read about these false prophets, I wonder what Bible they're studying. The Bible in my hands clearly says the date of our Lord's return is unknown and unknowable by anyone on earth.

- "Of that day and hour no one knows, not even the angels of heaven, but My Father only" (Matthew 24:36).

- "Watch therefore, for you do not know what hour your Lord is coming" (Matthew 24:42).
- "Therefore you also be ready, for the Son of Man is coming at an hour you do not expect" (Matthew 24:44).
- "Watch therefore, for you know neither the day nor the hour in which the Son of Man is coming" (Matthew 25:13).
- "But of that day and hour no one knows, not even the angels in heaven, nor the Son, but only the Father" (Mark 13:32).

Perhaps the last verse confuses you. If Jesus is God, why didn't He Himself know the time of His own return?

Well, when Jesus spoke those words, He had divested Himself of the independent use of His attributes. He had taken the form of a man (Philippians 2:7), totally obedient to His Father and completely reliant on the Holy Spirit. In His humanity, He had temporarily relinquished some of the privileges of His deity. When Jesus rose from the dead and received His glorified body, He once again had access to His omniscience. Therefore, Christ now knows and looks forward to the day of His return.

Why, then, would some people claim to know the timing of Jesus' return? If Christ Himself, in His humanity, didn't know the details, why would anyone else boast of knowing? That's the pull and power of deception.

Jesus warned us strenuously against being deceived in our spiritual lives. The New Testament epistles warn God's people about the possibility of being deceived no fewer than eleven times (Romans 16:18; 1 Corinthians 3:18; 6:9; 2 Corinthians 11:3; Galatians 6:7; Ephesians 5:6; Colossians 2:4; 2 Thessalonians 2:3; James 1:16, 22; 1 John 1:8).

Just as brilliant people have been scammed and taken in by clever hoaxes, it's also possible for Christians—even solid and mature believers—to be tricked. Without the wisdom and grace of God, we're all vulnerable to deception.

This danger will only accelerate as we move nearer to the World of the End.

## The Source of Deception in the World of the End

The spiritual deception of which Jesus warned isn't mere happenstance. There is a someone behind these deceptions. As I said earlier, Satan, the Enemy of our souls, is the ultimate deceiver and the father of lies. From the dawn of history, one of his primary tools has been deceit.

In the book of Revelation, John described Satan as "the great dragon . . . that serpent of old, called the Devil and Satan, who deceives the whole world" (12:9).

Jesus described Satan this way: "He was a murderer from the beginning, and does not stand in the truth, because there is no truth in him. When he speaks a lie, he speaks from his own resources, for he is a liar and the father of it" (John 8:44).

Spiritual deception may be Satan's most insidious weapon against those of us who follow Christ and belong to His church. Jesus and His apostles spoke of it nearly thirty times in the New Testament. Satan is a liar. He is the Serpent. He is the deceiver. But he masquerades as something else, and so do his devotees: "Such are false apostles, deceitful workers, transforming themselves into apostles of Christ. And no wonder! For Satan himself transforms himself into an angel of light" (2 Corinthians 11:13–14).

During his lifetime, pastor and theologian Dave Breese spoke often about the dangers of spiritual deception. He was especially aware of the subtlety of our adversary, writing, "We do well to remember that the cleverest liar makes statements that sound most nearly like the truth. . . . The most subtle created being in the universe is Lucifer. The cleverest set of lies he has ever produced is the satanic system of doctrine. With his doctrines, he presses quiet arguments upon reasonable men."[6]

When this deception becomes full-blown in the period surrounding the rapture, it will be unlike anything that has ever happened before on earth. Just as clouds gather before a storm, so we are feeling the pull of apocalyptic deception now. It's all around us. It's in the air!

What we're sensing are the birth pains of deception, which will intensify around the globe before the rapture occurs.

We feel it when politicians regularly fail to follow through on campaign promises. We feel it when media personalities tell us that up is down and dark is light. We feel it when scientists make outlandish claims about basic biology that don't stand up to common sense. We feel it when governments practice censorship in the name of protection and persecution in the name of peace. We feel it when social media entraps our children with its lies.

No wonder so many people distrust important institutions. As of May 2022:

- Only 42 percent of Americans have confidence in the government as a whole.
- About 35 percent have trust in Congress.
- An estimated 40 percent trust the news media, but that number drops to 28 percent for young adults.
- A third of Americans trust Wall Street and 26 percent trust Hollywood.
- Less than half of Americans—46 percent—trust their religious leaders.[7]

# DISTRUST OF INSTITUTIONS

**Only 42%** of Americans trust the government.   **Only 40%** of Americans trust the news media.   **Only 46%** of Americans trust religious leaders.

In short, we're already seeing an erosion of trust in the foundations that have held our cultures and civilizations together for millennia. That erosion will intensify as we approach the World of the End.

## The Strategy of Deception in the World of the End

About 2,400 years ago, a man in China by the name of Sun Tzu wrote a book called *The Art of War*. It remains popular today with leaders in business, entertainment, education, law, politics, government, sports, and many other fields who study and apply Tzu's principles in modern contexts.

Tzu wrote, "If you know the enemy and know yourself, you need not fear the result of a hundred battles. If you know yourself but not the enemy, for every victory gained you will also suffer a defeat. If you know neither the enemy nor yourself, you will succumb in every battle."[8]

Based on that paragraph, Sun Tzu is credited with coining the phrase, "Know your enemy."

This is what the apostle Paul had in mind when he told the Corinthians not to be "ignorant of [Satan's] devices" (2 Corinthians 2:11). As followers of Christ, we need to know our Enemy so we can stand against his schemes—including the scheme of deception. The best way to learn about Satan's strategies is by studying God's Word.

The strategy Satan implemented in the garden of Eden is the same he uses today, and the same he will leverage in the last days. Unfortunately, many Christians have never analyzed his strategy, which is one reason they're victimized by false prophets and deceptive doctrines running rampant.

What is Satan's universal strategy? It's presented in detail in the third chapter of Genesis.

## Satan Disputes God's Word

Satan began tempting Adam and Eve by disputing God's Word: "Now the serpent was more cunning than any beast of the field which the LORD God had made. And he said to the woman, 'Has God indeed said, "You shall not eat of every tree of the garden"?'" (Genesis 3:1).

Satan tried to water down what God had said. To change it. Just a little. He whispered in Eve's ear that she may not have heard God correctly.

The devil tries something similar on us today. We open the clear, plain Word of God in front of us and read a verse that tells us we shouldn't do something we'd really like to do. The next thing we know, someone shows up to give us an alternate interpretation of the text that will allow us to do what we know God has forbidden.

That is a moment of decision. We must choose to accept the truth of God's Word and act accordingly—or to allow ourselves to be deceived.

## Satan Denies God's Word

Next, Satan told Adam and Eve, "You will not surely die" (3:4).

The road from doubt to denial is not very long. When Satan said,

"You will not surely die," he was brazenly contradicting what God had said. See for yourself: "But of the tree of the knowledge of good and evil you shall not eat, for in the day that you eat of it you shall surely die" (2:17).

You can't miss the sequence! Doubt opens the door to denial. If Adam and Eve had not listened to Satan in the beginning, they would have never denied God in the end.

## Satan Displaces God's Word

After Satan disputed God's Word and then denied it, he displaced it. He told Adam and Eve: "You will be like God" (3:5). Satan was putting into their minds the same disturbing thought that had once entered his own mind—the same impulse that had transformed him from the anointed cherub to the devil of hell.

One of the easiest ways to see Satan's plan at work in the world today is to observe how our culture treats sin. How easily we seem to shift aside the pure truth of Scripture when doing so suits our purpose. Lying doesn't seem bad if we're trying to spare another person's feelings or when facing a case of situational ethics. Adultery doesn't feel as wrong when we describe it through doublespeak—just an "improper relationship" or even "true love." Gluttony and addiction aren't the result of personal choices but genetic disorders or chemical imbalances.

Soon we find ways to dispute what God's Word actually says. We say, "Those restrictions may have been true in the culture of Paul's day, but things are different now. A sophisticated modern person such as myself can handle a bit of gray instead of treating everything as black or white." When we allow Satan to sow doubts in our minds about the significance of sin, we've opened our hearts to the devil's deception.

How easily we justify our behavior! Right and wrong are turned upside down in the twinkling of an eye.

As Isaiah said, "Woe unto them that call evil good, and good evil; that put darkness for light, and light for darkness; that put bitter for sweet, and sweet for bitter!" (5:20 KJV).

That can easily happen if we allow ourselves to be deceived. But it doesn't have to. We don't have to let Satan control our lives. The apostle Paul's promise to the Corinthians still stands: "No temptation has overtaken you except such as is common to man; but God is faithful, who will not allow you to be tempted beyond what you are able, but with the temptation will also make the way of escape, that you may be able to bear it" (1 Corinthians 10:13).

## Satan Discounts God's Goodness

There's another link in the chain of deception. The devil wants us to discount the Lord's goodness, mercy, and grace.

Notice God's original instructions for humanity: "The LORD God commanded the man, saying, 'Of every tree of the garden you may freely eat; but of the tree of the knowledge of good and evil you shall not eat, for in the day that you eat of it you shall surely die'" (Genesis 2:16–17).

Do you see God's generosity? An abundance of goodness was offered "freely," with only one restriction. Yet Eve reframed God's original command when she spoke with Satan in Genesis 3: "The woman said to the serpent, 'We may eat the fruit of the trees of the garden'" (v. 2).

Do you see what's missing? Eve omitted God's gracious provision that she and Adam could "freely" eat of *every* tree in the garden. In other words, her comprehension of God's provision wasn't nearly as magnanimous as God intended. Satan had gotten to her with his evil insinuations about God.

When you start questioning the grace and goodness of God, you're on the road to deception.

Have you been tempted in that way? *Why did God let this happen?* you might wonder. *If God is so good, why are these things taking place? Will He not answer my prayer? Where is He?*

Let me give you some advice that has helped me in such times. Stop and ask yourself a few questions to get reoriented. *Is God good? Has He been good to me? Does His Word light the path ahead of me? Are His grace and provision sufficient for all my needs? Has He met my needs in the past? Has He given me promises to bear me through the difficulty?*

Yes, yes, and yes!

Don't allow Satan to push you into thinking God has abandoned or failed you. When you open the door to those kinds of thoughts, you'll let Satan sow seeds of deception in your heart.

### Satan Dramatizes God's Restrictions

Adam and Eve not only discounted God's goodness, but they also dramatized God's restrictions. Perhaps I should say they overdramatized God's restrictions—they added to them.

Nowhere in Genesis 1 and 2 do we find that God told the first humans not to "touch" the forbidden tree. But Eve said to the serpent, "We may eat the fruit of the trees of the garden; but of the fruit of the tree which is in the midst of the garden, God has said, 'You shall not eat it, nor shall you touch it, lest you die'" (Genesis 3:2–3).

What difference does that make? When you handle God's Word carelessly, you give Satan an inroad into your life. You'll soon be thinking less of the grace of God and more of the law of God. You'll be focused on what you *can't* do rather than what you are *privileged* to do.

That's how the Serpent deceives us. Throughout my entire career as a pastor, I've seen that demonic process played out. It happens to young people and older people, to new Christians and individuals who have been in the church for years, to the rich and the poor, to the highly educated and to high school dropouts.

When we overemphasize the boundaries in our lives, we are prone to misrepresenting God and His Word, and we fall into Satan's trap. The Bible tells each of us to be a "worker who does not need to be ashamed and who correctly handles the word of truth" (2 Timothy 2:15 NIV).

## Satan Diminishes God's Penalty

Adam and Eve discounted God's goodness, they dramatized God's restrictions, and finally they diminished God's penalty. Eve said, "Lest you die." But that's not what God said. Look again at Genesis 2:17: "But of the tree of the knowledge of good and evil you shall not eat, for in the day that you eat of it you shall surely die."

Eve left out the "surely die" part and changed it to a simpler "lest you die." The latter sounds like death is something that *might* happen—a possibility. The former makes it clear that death is inevitably connected with sin.

It's easy for modern Christians to start reading the Word of God in that fashion—to see "maybe" when the text says "definitely," or to hear "consider" when Scripture says "obey." It opens the door to the deception of Satan.

For example, have you noticed how the devil comes to a young person and whispers, "You know how you've got all these drives within you? God put them there. He never meant for you to be frustrated all the time. After all, everybody's doing it. We live in a sexually free environment, and yeah, I know you're a Christian—but you're also human. God expects you to be happy."

Listen, the devil doesn't want to help you! He wants to harm you. He wants to destroy, not build. He wants to enslave, not liberate. The Bible says, "The devil walks about like a roaring lion, seeking whom he may devour" (1 Peter 5:8). He seldom does this in an obvious or obnoxious way. He does it deceptively, by sowing little seeds of doubt about the Word of God.

Jesus said, "The thief does not come except to steal, and to kill, and to destroy" (John 10:10).

We must understand this reality as we look toward Christ's return. Satan is conducting a rampage of deception designed to destroy you and me. If we're not aware of it, we'll be victimized by it. And the momentum seems to be on his side because evil is accelerating to warp speed as we hurtle toward tribulation days.

## The Solution to Deception in the World of the End

A few years back, I read a story about an author named Mack Stiles who described leading a young man to faith in Christ. This particular young man, Andreas, was from Sweden, and the conversation got started when he voiced a common misconception about who Jesus is and what He offers.

Andreas said, "I've been told if I decide to follow Jesus, He will meet my needs and my life will get very good."

"No, Andreas, no!" said Stiles.

Andreas blinked with surprise.

"Actually, Andreas, you may accept Jesus and find that life goes very badly for you."

"What do you mean?" he asked.

"Well, you may find that your friends reject you, you could lose your job, your family might oppose your decision—there are a lot of bad things that may happen to you if you decide to follow Jesus. Andreas, when Jesus calls you, He calls you to go the way of the cross."

"Then why would I want to follow Jesus?"

The answer: "Andreas, because Jesus is true."[9]

Yes, and amen! That's the solution to our world being driven deeper and deeper into deception. That's the only needed answer to Satan's strategy of deceit.

Jesus is the truth, and He tells the truth. He is always, only, and forever true.

If you grasp the truth and it grasps you, it will set you free (John 8:32). That's the answer we need, and that is the answer Jesus provides. We know that because He told us, "I am the way, the truth, and the life" (John 14:6). Jesus is utterly dependable and trustworthy. You can take Him at His word. When you meet Him, you move from false to true, from deception to reality, from relative confusion to absolute knowledge.

Now, let's think as practically as we can. What can we do in our everyday lives to lift up the voice and the value of truth to a world drowning in deception?

## Seek the Truth

First, make up your mind to seek the truth wherever it leads.

Dr. Michael Guillen is a graduate of Cornell University with degrees in physics, math, and astronomy. He taught physics at Harvard and was science editor for ABC News. He was an atheist, but the complex precision of the universe shook his faith in atheism. He became fascinated with Buddhism, Islam, and Chinese mysticism, but they didn't satisfy him intellectually or emotionally.

One day his girlfriend, Laurel, asked him, "Have you ever actually read the Bible?"

For the next two years, Michael and Laurel read the Bible cover to cover. That led to a longer study of Scripture and a reevaluation of his worldview in light of the person of Jesus Christ. Michael was especially impressed with the prophetic portions of Scripture. "Among the hundreds of Old Testament prophecies are ones that foretell the coming of a Messiah," he wrote. "Those were fulfilled in Christ, and the logic of the New Testament became unassailable."

Dr. Guillen continued:

> One day it finally became clear to me what that conclusion had to be. It wasn't an emotional experience for me. Rather, it was the culmination of an intellectual dawning, a gradual awakening, that had begun two decades earlier at Cornell when I—an unkempt, malnourished scientific monk—asked myself a simple but pointed question: *How did this amazing, mostly invisible universe of ours come to be?* . . .
>
> The answer, I now concluded . . . had everything to do with the loving God who spoke them into being, and the resurrected Jesus who brought this loving but remote God down to Earth, making it possible for me—for you, for anyone—to know Him personally.[10]

Let me ask you the question Laurel asked Michael: Have you ever actually read the Bible? Do you study it? How are you handling it?

Psalm 119:160 says, "The entirety of Your word is truth."

The Bible: *need it, read it, heed it,* and *speed it* on its way to others. In other words, seek the truth.

## Speak the Truth

Next, speak the truth. Paul wrote, "Do not lie to one another, since you have put off the old man with his deeds, and have put on the new man who is renewed in knowledge according to the image of Him who created him" (Colossians 3:9–10).

Let's be frank. Many people feel comfortable with little lies. White lies. Minor misdirection.

- "Yes, the check's in the mail."
- "No, officer, I wasn't aware I was driving that fast."
- "I didn't think my friend would mind my using his account for that streaming service."
- "I didn't mean to."

As a culture, we've convinced ourselves dishonesty is only dangerous if it actively harms another person. But we're only fooling ourselves. Scripture says, "Lying lips are an abomination to the LORD, but those who deal truthfully are His delight" (Proverbs 12:22).

For that reason, let us speak the truth, the whole truth, and nothing but the truth.

## Show the Truth

Recently a sixty-seven-year-old woman was caught shoplifting in Stockholm. Her method was to place grocery items in a woven bag—a Christmas ham, meatballs, sausages, cheese, and more. Then, she attempted to leave the store while covering those items with another bag. The clerk noticed what the woman was doing and confronted her.

Now, here's the really strange part: the woman in question was one of the justices on Sweden's Supreme Court.

How should we process that news? On the one hand, this woman's crime was relatively minor. For many around the world, shoplifting is not a big deal. In California where I live, it's almost accepted or even expected that people will steal from stores and suffer no consequences! (Which is another deception, by the way.)

Yet because of this woman's status—because of her identity as a representative of the law in her nation's highest court—she had to resign from her lofty position.[11]

The solution to the devil's deception is for followers of Jesus to seek the truth, speak the truth, and, most importantly, show the truth through the witness of our everyday lives. Why? Because we are representatives of our Lord, who is the truth! Of course, representing Christ as the truth can be difficult when we live in a world that doesn't value or believe in "truth."

In his book *Time for Truth*, Dr. Os Guinness argued that the concept of truth in our modern world is dead: "Truth in any objective or absolute sense, truth that is independent of the mind of the knower, no longer exists. At best, truth is relative—it's all a matter of interpretation and it all depends on the perspective. At worst, truth is 'socially constructed'—merely a matter of human convention and a testament to the community that believes it and the power that established it."[12]

This is satanic! The devil has effectively inserted a false definition of *truth* into our culture, our schools, and yes, even into our churches.

But you cannot be a genuine Christ follower if you embrace a diluted form of truth. John MacArthur wrote, "Every true Christian should know and love the truth. Scripture says one of the key characteristics of 'those who perish' (people who are damned by their unbelief) is that 'they did not receive the love of the truth, that they might be saved' (2 Thessalonians 2:10)."[13]

Instead of diluting what is true, let's take Solomon's advice: "Buy the truth, and do not sell it" (Proverbs 23:23).

Here is another insight from Os Guinness:

All truth is God's truth and is true everywhere, for everyone, under all conditions. Truth is true in the sense that it is objective and independent of the mind of any human knower. . . .

Christian faith is not true because it works; it works because it is true. It is not true because we experience it; we experience it— deeply and gloriously—because it is true. It is not simply "true for us"; it is true for any who seek in order to find, because truth is true even if nobody believes it and falsehood is false even if everybody believes it. That is why truth does not yield to opinion, fashion, numbers, office, or sincerity—it is simply true and that is the end of it.[14]

The apostle John wrote, "I rejoiced greatly when brethren came and testified of the truth that is in you, just as you walk in the truth. I have no greater joy than to hear that my children walk in truth" (3 John vv. 3–4).

Let's *be* the truth. Let's stand against the things that are false by standing up for the things that are true. Let's stop posturing and actually be the people we want others to think we are.

This is what I know: as we ease into the deceptive days Jesus told us about in Matthew 24, the world is watching. It's time for us to *be honest*!

*"Behold, You desire truth in the inward
parts, and in the hidden part You will make
me to know wisdom" (Psalm 51:6).*

*"Buy the truth, and do not sell it" (Proverbs 23:23).*

*"Let your 'Yes' be 'Yes,' and your 'No,' 'No.' For whatever is
more than these is from the evil one" (Matthew 5:37).*

*"You shall know the truth, and the truth
shall make you free" (John 8:32).*

*"When He, the Spirit of truth, has come, He will
guide you into all truth" (John 16:13).*

*"Indeed, let God be true but every
man a liar" (Romans 3:4).*

*"Speaking the truth in love, we will grow to become
in every respect the mature body of him who is the
head, that is, Christ" (Ephesians 4:15 NIV).*

*"Let no corrupt word proceed out of your mouth, but
what is good for necessary edification, that it may
impart grace to the hearers" (Ephesians 4:29).*

*"Whatever things are true, whatever things are noble, whatever things are just, whatever things are pure, whatever things are lovely, whatever things are of good report, if there is any virtue and if there is anything praiseworthy— meditate on these things" (Philippians 4:8).*

*"I rejoiced greatly when brethren came and testified of the truth that is in you, just as you walk in the truth. I have no greater joy than to hear that my children walk in truth" (3 John vv. 3–4).*

# Chapter 3

# IN A WORLD OF WAR,
## *BE CALM*

*You will hear of wars and rumors of wars. See that
you are not troubled; for all these things must come
to pass, but the end is not yet. For nation will rise
against nation, and kingdom against kingdom.*

MATTHEW 24:6–7

If you ever visit the Karnak temple complex in Egypt, you'll view some of the oldest ruins in history, including decayed temples, chapels, and residences near Luxor. On the wall of one of the temples you'll see a set of Egyptian hieroglyphics that provides a description of the first recorded war in the history of the world. This wasn't the first conflict ever to occur, mind you, but it is the first known war to have been described in enduring written form.

The battle described by those hieroglyphics took place on April 16,

1457 BC, between Pharaoh Thutmose III and a large coalition of Canaanite tribes led by the king of Kadesh. Both armies boasted about ten thousand men. The Egyptians routed the Canaanite forces, who retreated to their walled city, known as Megiddo. The Egyptians besieged the city and took it seven months later.

What's interesting to me is the location of this war. I've already given you some clues, so take a guess. Exactly where did this battle happen?

The battle between Egypt and the Canaanites—the first recorded battle in world history—occurred in the Valley of Armageddon. This conflict is commonly called "the Battle of Megiddo."

I've visited the ruins of Megiddo many times when in Israel. From the top of Tel Megiddo, one views the vast Valley of Jezreel, also known as the Valley of Armageddon. Today it's the breadbasket of Israel, a perfect agricultural plain that yields huge amounts of barley, wheat, oranges, beans, watermelon, chickpeas, and sunflowers. But throughout history, that area has been the scene of countless conflicts—as many as two hundred battles.

It's from that exact spot that the Antichrist will set up his forward operating base in the final war of history (Revelation 16:16). The very name *Armageddon* comes from the Hebrew term *Har Megiddo*, or the "Mountain of Megiddo." Interestingly, Megiddo was not originally a mountain. It's an archaeological "tel," or manmade hill, that gained its height from the repeated destruction and rebuilding of the city.

I haven't words for the irony!

Our planet has a land surface of more than fifty-seven million square miles, yet the first and last recorded battles in history were (and will be) fought in the same place. These two wars serve as bookends, in a way, to the history of warfare. Between them is volume after volume of the bloody battles that mar the human story.

# Our Conflicts

In His message on the World of the End, Jesus warned that dissension would increase and that global warfare would envelop humanity in mounting measure. Standing on another high place—the Mount of Olives—He told His disciples, "You will hear of wars and rumors of wars. See that you are not troubled; for all these things must come to pass, but the end is not yet. For nation will rise against nation, and kingdom against kingdom" (Matthew 24:6–7).

Those words provide a springboard for us to examine three important ways our world has been, still is, and will be influenced by this phenomenon called war.

## The Curse of War

According to an article in the *New York Times*, the world has been at peace for only 268 of the past 3,400 years. In other words, only 8 percent of our history has been peaceful. No one knows how many people have perished in times of war. The *Times* speculated at least 108 million people were killed in wars in the twentieth century alone. Some experts believe a billion people have lost their lives during all the military conflicts that have pockmarked history like bomb craters.[1]

But casualties are only part of the story. Consider how many people have been bereaved by every single military death—mothers, fathers, wives, husbands, children, and friends. Even in our own lifetimes, we've stood by flag-draped coffins and listened to the mournful trumpets playing "Taps." Most of the soldiers slain have been young men, leading to decreasing birth rates and depressed populations. Also consider the maimed and wounded, those permanently traumatized, and all who have faced unspeakable atrocities. We can't conceive of the terror that accompanies the triumph of evil or the despair of defeat when it befalls good people.

War has terrible aftereffects, including famine and pestilence, as we'll see in subsequent chapters. When the Spanish adventurers invaded the empires in Mexico and Peru, they carried smallpox and measles that decimated local populations. Returning soldiers from World War I brought home the H1N1 virus, which infected a third of the world's population and killed more people than the war itself.

C. S. Lewis knew the curse of war. During World War I he served on the front lines in France and was wounded by an exploding shell.

Years later, when World War II arrived, he wrote:

> My memories of the last war haunted my dreams for years. Military service, to be plain, includes the threat of every temporal evil; pain and death which is what we fear from sickness: isolation from those we love which is what we fear from exile: toil under arbitrary masters . . . which is what we fear from slavery: hunger, thirst, and exposure which is what we fear from poverty. I'm not a pacifist. If it's got to be, it's got to be. But the flesh is weak and selfish and I think death would be much better than to live through another war.[2]

So here we are, a few billion souls occupying a small, spinning planet, surrounded by a stunning universe and inhabiting a world of unrivaled beauty. Yet our history is soaked with blood, saturated with sorrow, and dominated by massive armies that now have the potential to unleash worldwide carnage.

Yes, war *is* a horrible thing, but sometimes it is a very necessary thing. I will never forget the first time I read the following statement:

> War is an ugly thing, but not the ugliest of things: the decayed and degraded state of moral and patriotic feeling, which thinks

nothing is *worth* a war, is worse. . . . A man who has nothing which he . . . cares more about than he does about his personal safety, is a miserable creature, who has no chance of being free, unless he is made and kept so by the exertions of better men than himself.[3]

Consider this: war produces heroes and brings out the best in those whose cause is right. Without just wars, evil cannot be hindered. The Hitlers of history would not be stopped. Dictators would prevail.

War, then, is a paradox.

Dr. Margaret MacMillan, an expert on the history of warfare, wrote:

It is another uncomfortable truth about war that it brings both destruction and creation. So many of our advances in science and technology—the jet engine, transistors, computers—came about because they were needed in wartime. Penicillin, which has saved so many lives, was first discovered in 1928 by Sir Alexander Fleming but the funds to develop it were not available until the Second World War. The Canadian doctor Norman Bethune pioneered blood transfusions on the battlefield. The practice of triage, now common in emergency rooms in hospitals, started in wars. . . . Surgery—for traumatic wounds or to rebuild shattered faces— made huge advances during the wars of the twentieth century.[4]

Some of history's greatest moments have reflected the courage of leaders in times of war. Who is not moved by Churchill's stirring words that represent one of the greatest moments of leadership in the modern world? "Let us therefore brace ourselves to our duties, and so bear ourselves that, if the British Empire and its Commonwealth last for a thousand years, men will still say, 'This was their finest hour.'"[5]

Churchill's gravelly voice was one of England's greatest weapons as he told his people with resolute courage, "We shall not flag or fail.

We shall go on to the end, we shall fight in France, we shall fight on the seas and oceans, we shall fight with growing confidence and growing strength in the air, we shall defend our Island, whatever the cost may be, we shall fight on the beaches, we shall fight on the landing grounds, we shall fight in the fields and in the streets, we shall fight in the hills; we shall never surrender."[6]

The conflict between good and evil, which each of us feels in our own souls, finds its greatest field of operation on the battlegrounds of war. Human history, with all its triumphs and tragedies, has been ushered from one lurching moment to another by warfare.

## The Cause of War

Because the curse of war is so great, philosophers have long searched for its cause. Why do people fight one another? Why does nation rise against nation and kingdom against kingdom? Svetlana Alexievich, a Belarusian journalist, wrote, "War remains, as it always has been, one of the chief human mysteries."[7]

Dr. MacMillan wrote, "The evidence seems to be on the side of those who say that human beings, as far back as we can tell, have had a propensity to attack each other in organized ways—in other words, to make war. That challenges us to understand why it is that human beings are willing and able to kill each other."[8]

Why indeed?

The ancients believed the Trojan War started when Zeus concluded there were too many people on earth and prompted humans to fight and kill one another. Others point to Darwin's theory of evolution and his concept of the survival of the fittest.

But we cannot blame the reality of war on mythical gods or evolutionary schemes.

One of the most chilling books on this subject, *Ordinary Men* by Christopher R. Browning, describes how a unit of average, middle-aged, working-class German men became cold-blooded murderers able to kill without remorse. Not only did these soldiers commit mass murder, but they also rounded up Jewish people for deportation to the death camps. Browning's disturbing thesis is that almost any of us is capable of committing such atrocities if we're caught up in an environment that alters moral norms, creates group dynamics, and defers to authority.

In short, the cause of war is the human heart, and we can trace the problem back to the moment Adam and Eve first disobeyed God. The vertical rupture sin caused in our relationship with the Lord produced a corresponding horizontal rupture between one person and another.

First, Adam and Eve hid from God, then Cain killed Abel. From that day forward, history and the pages of the Bible have been marked by warfare. In fact, in the Old Testament, the word *war* occurs more than three hundred times. More than two hundred times in the Old Testament, Jehovah is called "the LORD of hosts." After Moses and the children of Israel escaped the clutches of Pharaoh through the intervention of Jehovah, they sang this song of victory: "The LORD is a man of war; the LORD is His name" (Exodus 15:3).

Many of God's great servants were military men: Saul, David, Moses, Gideon, and many of the kings of Israel. This was the testimony of King David: "Blessed be the LORD my Rock, who trains my hands for war, and my fingers for battle" (Psalm 144:1).

People often assume that war is common in the Old Testament but scarcely mentioned in the New Testament. That's not the case. Whenever a soldier appears in the New Testament record, for example, he is given commendation and appreciation. The apostles used the language of war on many occasions to illustrate the believer's journey. They spoke of "desires for pleasure that war in your members" (James 4:1). They instructed their followers to "abstain from fleshly lusts which war against the soul" (1 Peter 2:11). They were told that through Christ, they could become "conquerors" (Romans 8:37). Timothy was encouraged by Paul to "wage the good warfare" (1 Timothy 1:18). These are just a few of such uses.

I think it is safe to say that because of the conflict between good and evil that originated in the garden of Eden, war has become a major theme in the human story—and will remain so up to and through the World of the End.

## The Course of War

Having looked at the curse and the cause of war, let's look at its course. As I indicated, human conflict started with Adam and Eve and Cain and Abel. Throughout history, the technology of war has advanced until this moment, when the world has produced enough firepower to kill everyone on earth many times over.

That brings us again to the words of Jesus in Matthew 24: "You will hear of wars and rumors of wars. See that you are not troubled; for all these things must come to pass, but the end is not yet. For nation will rise against nation, and kingdom against kingdom" (vv. 6–7).

Remember earlier when I said there have been only a few years in world history without national and international conflict? Some of those years occurred during the lifetime of Jesus, when the world experienced a time of relative tranquility. This was the golden age of Roman life, when the arts, literature, and technology advanced to heights not previously seen. The Roman Empire ruled a quarter of the world's population.

In that season, few people would have predicted the return and acceleration of global conflict, but Jesus knew what was ahead. He unequivocally told His disciples, "You will hear of wars."

He also told them they would hear of "rumors of wars." That word *rumors* is a translation of the original Greek term *akoe*. It can mean either "report" or "sound." If Jesus intended the former, He was telling

His disciples they would hear of actual wars and of reports of others that couldn't be verified.

But many experts believe the better translation is "sound" or "noise."

In other words, you will hear about wars far away, and you will actually hear the sounds of wars close by. Those wars will come to you, to your gates, to your cities. The Good News Translation says, "You are going to hear the noise of battles close by and the news of battles far away" (Matthew 24:6). One commentary said, "'Wars and rumors of war' can mean wars and threats of war, wars near and far, or wars and impending wars."[9]

Biblical scholars believe the phrase "wars and rumors of wars" represent the earliest description of world war: "This expression is a Hebrew idiom for a world war. Jesus's statement here is that when a world war occurs, rather than merely a local war, that world war would signal that the end of the age had begun."[10]

Whatever the case, the idea is there will be wars everywhere, which will increase in intensity, scope, and fearfulness as the age draws toward its God-ordained conclusion.

As I'm writing this, the Russian invasion of Ukraine slogs on with heartbreaking images on television every night. Vladimir Putin has amassed the world's largest collection of nuclear weapons and has threatened to "use them, if needed."[11]

China is surrounding Taiwan with warships as the Communist government conducts war games and drills. China expert Evan Osnos argues that China is "preparing to shape the twenty-first century, much as the U.S. shaped the twentieth."[12] Another China watcher, Rush Doshi, wrote, "China now poses a challenge unlike any the United States has ever faced."[13]

Both Pakistan and India possess nuclear weapons, and the wrong provocation at the wrong time could spell disaster.

At this time, nine countries are known to possess nuclear weapons, and the global inventory is estimated at thirteen thousand weapons. According to experts, "The warheads on just *one* US nuclear-armed submarine have seven times the destructive power of all the bombs dropped during World War II, including the two atomic bombs dropped on Japan." Yes, you read that correctly. On just one submarine! And currently there are ten such American submarines prowling the world's oceans.[14]

But the oceans are filled with submarines from other nations too, all carrying equal payloads. A new arms race has begun with nearly all nuclear powers working overtime to increase their arsenals. China has an estimated 350 nuclear warheads, with approximately 100 assigned to missiles capable of reaching the United States.

The United Kingdom has 120 nuclear weapons, with "forty deployed at any given time" on Trident submarines. France has "nearly 300 deployed nuclear weapons," most on submarines.

North Korea has enough nuclear material for up to forty weapons, and some experts believe half of those have already been assembled.

# COUNTRIES WITH NUCLEAR WEAPONS

| Countries | Estimated Number of Nuclear Weapons |
|---|---|
| Russia | 5,977 |
| United States | 5,428 |
| China | 350 |
| France | 290 |
| United Kingdom | 225 |
| Pakistan | 165 |
| India | 160 |
| Israel | 90 |
| North Korea | 20 |

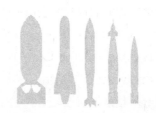

"Status of World Nuclear Forces," Federation of American Scientists, accessed May 19, 2022, https://fas.org/issues/nuclear-weapons/status-world-nuclear-forces/.

Israel rarely discusses its nuclear capability, but it faces an existential threat from the apocalyptic Islamic rulers of Iran who vow to destroy the Jewish state.[15] We can be sure Israel is well armed and ready to respond.

It's only the grace of God that has thus far prevented a terrorist group from detonating a nuclear device somewhere on earth, perhaps in a city near you.

Time won't allow me to discuss biological weapons and other terrors. Were all the weapons on earth deployed and detonated at the same time, it's likely the earth itself would be reduced to a charred ball of burnt carbon.

I don't believe that's going to happen, because the Lord has given us a glimpse into the future in Matthew 24 and in the book of Revelation. Any moment now, Jesus is going to come for His church, and the events described in Matthew 24 that have been growing in intensity and frequency will give birth to a series of wars like nothing ever before witnessed in human history, finally reaching their zenith at Armageddon.

But the Bible says that war will be suddenly interrupted by the majestic return of Christ, from whose mouth will proceed a sharp sword (Revelation 19:11–21). He will save His people from annihilation, save the world from total destruction, and establish a kingdom where peace and justice will reign supreme.

In other words, as terrifying as our current world conflicts may seem, we can take solace in the truth that the course of war will eventually lead us to Christ.

## Our Confidence

Jesus summarized all these ideas when He warned of "wars and rumors of wars." But it's what He next said that seems most surprising.

We would have expected Him to say, "You will hear of wars and rumors of wars, so be prepared for trouble. Keep an anxious eye on the times. Expect to feel uneasy and prepare for the many foes and woes to come."

But no; that's not what He said. Our Lord told us, "You will hear of wars and rumors of wars. See that you are not troubled" (Matthew 24:6).

The Greek word for "be troubled" means to be terrified, to cry aloud, to scream. Jesus was telling us not to panic, even when we are surrounded by wars and rumors of war. How is that possible? The answer is wrapped up in the peace we can find from God's promise, God's presence, and God's plan.

## Peace from God's Promise

First, we can choose to be "not troubled" by the reality of war because God has promised that, one day, war will no longer be a reality. War will cease. Like you, I feel grieved by the conflicts that harm and destroy so many, especially so many innocent people. We may ask good questions about why these things happen. But the day is coming when Psalm 46 will be fulfilled: "He makes wars cease to the end of the earth" (v. 9).

Isaiah spoke of the days of Jesus' coming kingdom when He will reign from Jerusalem, and all the tribes of the earth will hear His teachings and learn His ways. "They shall beat their swords into plowshares, and their spears into pruning hooks; nation shall not lift up sword against nation, neither shall they learn war anymore" (Isaiah 2:4).

Dr. M. R. DeHaan wrote of this day:

The Bible is replete with prophecies of a coming age of peace and prosperity. It will be a time when war will be utterly unknown. Not a single armament plant will be operating, not a soldier or sailor will be in uniform, no military camps will exist, and not one cent will be spent for armaments of war, not a single penny will be used for defense, much less for offensive warfare. Can you imagine such an age, when all nations shall be at perfect peace, all the resources available for enjoyment, all industry engaged in the articles of a peaceful luxury?[16]

We have not yet reached that day, but God has promised that we will reach it. In the meantime, though there is warfare in the world, there can be peace in the hearts of God's children.

## Peace from God's Presence

Nothing is more important, or more confidence boosting, than the promise that God will be with us during difficult seasons—including conflicts of all kinds. Here are just a few of those promises.

- "Do not let your heart faint, do not be afraid . . . for the LORD your God is He who goes with you, to fight for you against your enemies, to save you" (Deuteronomy 20:3–4).
- "The LORD, He is the One who goes before you. He will be with you, He will not leave you nor forsake you; do not fear nor be dismayed" (Deuteronomy 31:8).
- "As I was with Moses, so I will be with you. I will not leave you nor forsake you. . . . Have not I commanded you? Be strong and of good courage; do not be afraid, nor be dismayed, for the LORD your God is with you wherever you go" (Joshua 1:5, 9).
- "When you pass through the waters, I will be with you" (Isaiah 43:2).
- "He Himself has said, 'I will never leave you nor forsake you.' So we may boldly say: 'The LORD is my helper; I will not fear. What can man do to me?'" (Hebrews 13:5–6).

The promise of the presence of God in our lives is so important that when He sent His Son into our world to provide for our salvation, one of the names He was given celebrates His presence with us: "'Behold, the virgin shall be with child, and bear a Son, and they shall call His name Immanuel,' which is translated, 'God with us'" (Matthew 1:23).

Jim and Marina Noyes were in Ukraine when Russia invaded. They spent the first ten days of the war in Kyiv, where they had planted a church. They wanted to stay in Ukraine, but they had two grandchildren, and one is a special-needs child. She is a little girl who uses a walker to move about. One day Marina heard the child talking to her baby doll in Ukrainian. She said, "Do not worry. Don't panic, sweetie. All will be well. Mommy is with you."

From the lips of children!

Jim and Marina, their son and daughter-in-law, and the two children wound their way around the conflict to escape Ukraine. When Jim and Marina arrived in the United States, they shared their story.

"When the trouble comes, we cry," said Marina, speaking on behalf of the Ukrainian people. "When it gets bad, we pray. When it becomes unbearable, we sing." She said that Ukrainians have written thousands of songs since the war began. "Ukraine has always been religious," she added, "but now Ukraine is really turning to God."[17]

Our peace amid conflict—our ability to sing in the storm—comes from the One who said, "Let not your heart be troubled, neither let it be afraid" (John 14:27). He is the same Savior who told us, "In the world you will have tribulation; but be of good cheer, I have overcome the world" (16:33).

## Peace from God's Plan

Let's look at Matthew 24:6–7 one more time: "You will hear of wars and rumors of wars. See that you are not troubled; for all these things must come to pass, but the end is not yet. For nation will rise against nation, and kingdom against kingdom."

*All these things must come to pass.*

I love it when Jesus says, "Must." It indicates the indisputable, inexorable decrees of the almighty God in things large and small that must and will be fulfilled. Because Jesus knows the things that "must" be fulfilled, we can rest in Him and abide in His peace—whatever our world may be doing and wherever it may be spinning.

In late 2021, a two-man Youth For Christ team from Lebanon went to eastern Sudan to help organize the YFC work there and evangelize rural areas. John Sagherian was a seventy-four-year-old widower. Elie Heneine, twenty-seven, was a newly married YFC worker.

John and Elie met at the hotel early on their first day to begin their work. Noticing everyone gathered around a television, they learned the military had staged an overnight coup in the capital of Khartoum. Sudan was in crisis—again. The airports were restricted, and the population was tense.

Instantly, everything the two men had planned was up in the air. Elie's wife back in Lebanon kept them up-to-date on the news she was hearing, and it seemed impossible for their mission to continue. But they determined to do their best.

Two days before the coup, John wanted to meet a man named Sabet, who showed leadership potential and had recruited others to help him in evangelism. So John and Elie made their way to the meeting spot and found thirty people on plastic chairs in a three-walled, tin-roofed structure.

John had a message he often preached, so he pulled out his Bible and preached it. The title was "Why Is God Doing This to Us?" He reassured the congregation that God had a plan, even in the midst of troubles and conflicts. Rather than becoming angry and bitter, we should look to see what He is doing.

Our constant question to God, he said, is, "What now, Lord?"

The day of the coup, Sabet took John and Elie in a three-wheeled auto rickshaw to meet thirty-five church leaders. The rickshaw was packed with five other passengers and a baby goat. The driver was fifteen. They navigated around riots and areas of protest. Finally arriving at their destination, John preached from Psalm 78 to the youth workers.

Conditions in eastern Sudan worsened. The government cut off phone and internet service across the nation. Just as John and Elie decided to return home, the airports closed.

What now, Lord?

Near them was a school in a poor village. Ninety-five percent of the students were Muslim, but the headmaster was a Christian, a man whom Sabet had led to the Lord ten years earlier. This man had won a few others to Christ, gathered them into his home, and started a church. Now, in the middle of a national crisis, the same headmaster gathered all the students to a rally and told John to preach to them about Jesus.

Having been a Youth For Christ worker for decades, John was eager to speak—and to give an altar call. Based on his experience, he thought a hundred students would show up and perhaps five or so would be saved. Instead, over a thousand students showed up on the schoolyard grounds. John preached the gospel and explained the way of eternal salvation provided by Jesus. Then he asked anyone wanting to give their life to Christ to stand.

The crowd was nervous, but eventually one person stood. Then a second, a third, and a fourth. Before long, the entire student body was standing. Thinking they had misunderstood, John had everyone sit while he explained the importance of this decision. This time he asked those who wanted to follow Christ to raise their hands. Eighty percent of the students did so.

John and Elie finally made their way back to Lebanon, but I like the way Elie summed up the trip: "God moved circumstances and people, putting us in places we couldn't have imagined. It was like a well-played chess match, and God won."[18]

On a certain level, all of human history appears to be a chess match between God and the devil, but there's no question about who has won, is winning, and who will always secure the victory.

That's why Jesus told us we'd hear of wars and rumors of war— but not to be troubled! The only way to do that is by faith—to trust in Jesus Christ.

Isaiah said it this way: "You will keep him in perfect peace, whose mind is stayed on You" (Isaiah 26:3).

I like what Paul David Tripp wrote:

> Peace is found in trusting the person who controls all the things that you don't understand and who knows no mystery because he has planned it all. How do you experience this remarkable peace? . . . You experience it by keeping your mind stayed on the Lord.
>
> The more you meditate on his glory, his power, his wisdom, his grace, his faithfulness, his righteousness, his patience, his zeal to redeem, and his commitment to his eternal promises to you, the more you can deal with mystery in your life. It really is true that peace in times of trouble is not found in figuring out your life, but in worship of the One who has everything figured out already.[19]

Trust the Lord Jesus Christ with your soul's salvation. Trust the Lord Jesus with your struggles and sorrows. Trust Jesus with your service. He has work for you to do in these last days. And when you hit roadblocks, end up in rickshaws, and find yourself in the midst of conflict, just ask, "What now, Lord?" He wants to use you more than you know, and He can do far more than all you can ask or imagine (Ephesians 3:20).

Yes, we will hear of dissension, of wars and rumors of war, but don't be troubled. These things must happen, but Jesus is coming—right on schedule!

Bruce Belfrage was an English actor who became a reporter and news reader for the British Broadcast Company. As the Battle of Britain terrorized London during World War II, the German Luftwaffe bombed the city with unremitting air raids. The BBC headquarters were not spared.

On the evening of October 15, 1940, the BBC took a direct hit from a 500-pound, delayed-reaction German bomb, which exploded during the nine o'clock news. Seven people were killed. Bruce Belfrage was reading the news at that very moment, even as plaster, soot, and smoke rained down on him. To everyone's amazement, Belfrage didn't miss a beat. He calmly kept reading the news as if nothing had happened. The only thing listeners at home heard was a dull thud and someone whispering, "Are you all right?"

Belfrage's only comment was, "Carry on. It's all right."[20]

That's what Jesus was telling us in Matthew 24:6–7. Even in a war-weary world, we need to keep calm and carry on.

I'll sum it up like this: we live in a world that will war from Armageddon to Armageddon, but we serve a Lord who reigns from everlasting to everlasting (Psalm 90:2).

Let not your heart be troubled!

Trust Christ and carry on. *Be calm.*

*"Do not let your heart faint, do not be afraid, and do not tremble or be terrified because of them; for the Lord your God is He who goes with you, to fight for you against your enemies, to save you" (Deuteronomy 20:3–4).*

*"As I was with Moses, so I will be with you. I will not leave you nor forsake you. . . . Have not I commanded you? Be strong and of good courage; do not be afraid, nor be dismayed, for the Lord your God is with you wherever you go" (Joshua 1:5, 9).*

*"Some trust in chariots, and some in horses; but we will remember the name of the Lord our God" (Psalm 20:7).*

*"Though an army may encamp against me, my heart shall not fear; though war may rise against me, in this I will be confident. One thing I have desired of the Lord, that will I seek: that I may dwell in the house of the Lord all the days of my life" (Psalm 27:3–4).*

*"He makes wars cease to the end of the earth; He breaks the bow and cuts the spear in two; He burns the chariot in the fire. Be still, and know that I am God; I will be exalted among the nations, I will be exalted in the earth!" (Psalm 46:9–10).*

*"Blessed be the Lord my Rock, who trains my hands for war, and my fingers for battle—my lovingkindness and my fortress, my high tower and my deliverer, my shield and the One in whom I take refuge" (Psalm 144:1–2).*

*"The horse is prepared for the day of battle, but deliverance is of the LORD" (Proverbs 21:31).*

*"You will keep him in perfect peace, whose mind is stayed on You" (Isaiah 26:3).*

*"Peace I leave with you, My peace I give to you; not as the world gives do I give to you. Let not your heart be troubled, neither let it be afraid" (John 14:27).*

*"In everything by prayer and supplication, with thanksgiving, let your requests be made known to God; and the peace of God, which surpasses all understanding, will guard your hearts and minds through Christ Jesus" (Philippians 4:6–7).*

## Chapter 4

# IN A WORLD OF DISASTERS,
## *BE CONFIDENT*

*There will be famines, pestilences, and*
*earthquakes in various places.*
MATTHEW 24:7

Have you ever wanted to visit a distant planet? Or to feel like you're on one? Then take a vacation to Yellowstone National Park. The terrain is otherworldly, and in places you'll feel like you're on the set of a science fiction movie.

More than ten thousand hydrothermal spots bubble up in Yellowstone—geysers, mud pots, steam vents, fumaroles, and hot springs. The Grand Prismatic Spring is a scalding, multicolored pond larger than a football field. At the center you'll see deep blue hues encircled by green and yellow bands, with lots of orange along the outskirts. The colors are caused by different species of heat-loving bacteria. Steam rising from the pond yields an eerie feeling. The ground around the pool resembles piecrust.

When touring Yellowstone, it pays to remember you're walking across the top of an active supervolcano that has erupted several times in the past. Every moment of every day, teams from different universities, geological societies, and federal agencies are monitoring the area's seismic activity.

In 2021 alone, 2,773 earthquakes were recorded in the Yellowstone area.[1] As reporter Brad Plumer explained, "Lurking beneath Yellowstone National Park is a reservoir of hot magma five miles deep, fed by a gigantic plume of molten rock welling up from hundreds of miles below."[2]

What would happen if the volcano blew? Plumer wrote that a major eruption "could spew ash for thousands of miles . . . damaging buildings, smothering crops, and shutting down power plants." The states of Wyoming, Montana, Idaho, and Colorado would be buried in three feet of volcanic ash, which is "a mix of splintered rock and glass."[3]

Such an eruption would make "Mount St. Helens look like a hiccup."[4]

Some geologists believe clouds of poisonous ash could spread across the United States and Canada with the force of a hurricane. The ash could shred lungs, collapse roofs, take down transformers, and threaten the nation's power grid. It could create a superwinter that would last a decade.

I'm not discouraging you from visiting Yellowstone. Scientists aren't predicting eruptions anytime soon, and every family should show their children, if possible, what God has wrought in this stunning corner of Wyoming.

And yet . . .

When I read descriptions from God's Word about what will one day happen, and when I remember there are at least twelve other supervolcanoes around the globe, I can't help being reminded of scenes from the book of Revelation. Natural disasters will be part of the tribulation, but they aren't confined to the end of history. According to our Lord's message on Olivet, these elements—earthquakes, famines, plagues, disasters—will continue to increase in intensity and frequency as we move closer to the ultimate day of our Lord's return.

That brings us to our Lord's next prediction in Matthew 24.

As we've already seen, the World of the End will be a difficult and dangerous place—one defined by destruction, deceit, and war. Jesus' prophecy makes that clear. As we move to verse 7 in His Olivet Discourse, we see a repetition of Jesus' earlier promise about wars and rumors of wars: "Nation will rise against nation," He reiterated, "and kingdom against kingdom."

It's the second half of verse 7 that should cause us to review our insurance policies. According to Christ, "There will be famines, pestilences, and earthquakes in various places."

In other words, the World of the End will increasingly be filled with devastation and disaster along with all their ensuing effects.

## Global Disasters Are Unavoidable

"Wait a minute," you say. "There have always been natural disasters in human history. Every century has endured famine, pestilence, and earthquakes. So how can natural disasters be a prophecy or a sign for the World of the End?"

The answer lies in the birth-pains principle I mentioned earlier. None of Jesus' prophetic promises from the Olivet Discourse will be unique to the end of history. What *will* be unique is the frequency and intensity with which those events will impact our world. The closer we get to the final chapter of human civilization, the more we'll experience the inescapable dangers Jesus predicted in Matthew 24.

## Famines

Standing on the Mount of Olives, Jesus used a frightening word—one that, to His disciples, recalled a host of Old Testament stories: "There will be famines" (Matthew 24:7).

As they listened to our Lord's message, perhaps Peter, James, John, and Andrew recalled the famine that sent the Israelites to Egypt at the end of Genesis. Or the famine that drove Naomi and her family to Moab in the book of Ruth. They might have thought of the famine triggered in Elijah's day when God withheld rain from Israel for three and a half years.

The prophet Jeremiah anticipated the signs of the times when he linked war, famine, and plague in Jeremiah 14:12, saying: "I will consume them by the sword, by the famine, and by the pestilence." Remember what Jesus said in Matthew 24:7: "Nation will rise against nation, and kingdom against kingdom. And there will be famines, pestilences."

Once again, Jesus' words dovetail seamlessly with the seal judgments recorded in Revelation 6. In John's prophetic vision, the fiery red horse of warfare is followed by the black horse of famine and the pale horse of death.

Jesus and the writers of the Bible understood the recurring patterns of history: sword, famine, and pestilence.

So do today's humanitarians. The Global Hunger Index, which is compiled and published by European humanitarian organizations, actually used language from Revelation 6 to describe current conditions in our world. In an online report called "Armed Conflict and the Challenge of Hunger," the Index revealed that "war and famine, two fearsome horsemen, have long ridden side by side. Armed conflict disrupts food systems, destroys livelihoods, displaces people, and leaves those who do not flee both terrified and unsure when they will eat their next meal."

The report continued:

Today's famines are "complex humanitarian emergencies," caused mostly by armed conflict and exacerbated by natural disasters or international policies....These "new wars"...involve not only state armies and insurgents, but also paramilitaries and ethnic militia, criminal gangs, mercenaries, and international forces. Most new wars are civil wars, which increasingly spill over borders, disrupt livelihoods and food systems, and force people to flee.

The writers of the report then made this keen observation: "Hunger is somehow different from other human stresses. Food and famine strike a deep emotive chord, even among people who have never personally faced starvation. Around the world, people believe that a government that cannot feed its people has forfeited its legitimacy."[5]

One example staring us in the face is Ukraine. Prior to Russia's invasion of Ukraine, those two nations together produced about 30 percent of the world's supply of grain.[6] The war has disrupted Ukraine, threatening to push another forty-seven million people into extreme hunger. I even heard a recent report warning that the crisis will go on for years.[7]

I realize many of us have food in our pantries, and few of us miss any meals. But hunger does lurk near the surface in America; many children go to school each morning with empty stomachs. One organization found that nearly 1.5 million New York City residents face food insecurity, including one in four children.[8] According to *The Hill*, about 14 percent of America's military families are food insecure.[9]

I'm not a fan of much of what happens with the globalists at Davos. But at the last meeting of the World Economic Forum, Kristalina Georgieva, the International Monetary Fund managing director, said something relevant to this subject: "'The anxiety about access to food at a reasonable price globally is hitting the roof' as food prices continue 'to go up up up.'"[10]

These developments have surprised the leaders of our day, but Jesus saw them coming. We can trust what the Bible says about the future, including the increase in famines as we approach the World of the End.

## Plagues

Jesus went on in Matthew 24:7 to say, "And there will be . . . pestilences." The Greek word Matthew used is *loimos*. That term doesn't describe minor maladies or seasonal sicknesses. Rather, the pestilences Jesus predicted are huge in scale and impact. They will sweep over large regions of the world and be difficult to control.

Interestingly, there's a strong connection between famine and pestilence in Scripture. For example:

- In describing the curses that would befall the nation of Israel if they rejected God, Moses wrote, "They shall be wasted with hunger, devoured by pestilence and bitter destruction" (Deuteronomy 32:24).
- Threatened by enemies, King Jehoshaphat of Judah declared his faith in God by saying, "If disaster comes upon us—sword, judgment, pestilence, or famine—we will stand before this temple and in Your presence (for Your name is in this temple), and cry out to You in our affliction, and You will hear and save" (2 Chronicles 20:9).

This isn't a random connection. War results in food shortages. Whenever food is scarce, people become nutritionally deprived. Their health suffers, which creates an environment for disease to flourish.

Global pandemics have been relatively rare in history. The plague of Justinian likely killed between 30 to 50 million people in the sixth century.[11] "The bubonic plague resulted in approximately 200 million deaths in the 14th century."[12] And there were other, lesser plagues that ravaged different regions of the world throughout the centuries that followed. But large-scale episodes of pestilence have been few and far between.

In our lifetime, however, the world has become interconnected. The twentieth century began with the Spanish flu pandemic, which killed more than 40 million people around the world. The Asian flu and the Hong Kong flu both resulted in more than a million deaths in the 1950s and 1960s, respectively. The HIV/AIDS epidemic has brought an additional 35 million deaths and is still raging. In the twenty-first century, we have already seen swine flu, SARS, MERS, Ebola—and yes, COVID-19.[13]

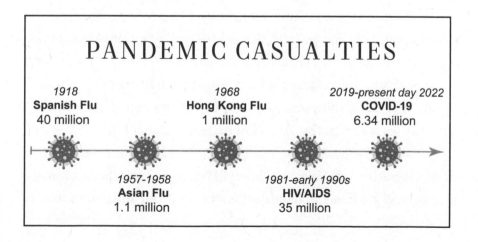

PANDEMIC CASUALTIES

1918
**Spanish Flu**
40 million

1968
**Hong Kong Flu**
1 million

2019-present day 2022
**COVID-19**
6.34 million

1957-1958
**Asian Flu**
1.1 million

1981-early 1990s
**HIV/AIDS**
35 million

After our experience with the coronavirus, none of us knows what may escape from a laboratory somewhere in the world or what disease may next sweep the globe.

Had I been with Jesus, I might have thought advancing medical progress would eradicate disease, given enough time in history. But He knew differently. In a world of increasing medical miracles, disease has not been eliminated or eradicated. Instead, sickness is more prevalent than ever, and the trend lines are terrifying.

## Earthquakes

The next sign Jesus predicted seems out of order. We see the connection between war, famine, pandemics, and death. But earthquakes? They are random. Unlike war, they aren't caused by human means. Unlike famines, they seldom offer warnings or explanations. Unlike pestilence, earthquakes come suddenly, demolish in an instant, and leave only aftershocks.

When God created the world, He designed it with a molten core made of boiling magma, covered by a mantle nearly two thousand miles deep. Atop that, our surface lands and seas rest on tectonic plates, which sometimes shift. Scientists are still working to understand those shifts and how they impact our world. But God has understood those forces from day one. More than that, He is in control even of our earth's chaotic core.

One day an ultimate global earthquake will bring down the cities of the world, including Babylon, the city of the Antichrist. This will occur as Jesus returns at the end of history.

According to Revelation 16:18, when the angel pours out the final bowl of wrath on the world, there will be "a great earthquake, such a mighty and great earthquake as had not occurred since men were on the earth."

Isaiah 2:19 says, "They shall go into the holes of the rocks, and into the caves of the earth, from the terror of the LORD and the glory of His majesty, when He arises to shake the earth mightily."

When Jesus died on Calvary, the ground of Jerusalem quaked (Matthew 27:50–54). That's nothing compared to what will happen when He returns. For now, as we've learned, we're suffering early birth pains, and we never know when we'll awaken to news of a major quake in some part of the world.

Just today, as I sat down to work on this chapter, I was told of an earthquake in Afghanistan that killed at least a thousand people. Reports said it was the deadliest earthquake there in two decades.[14]

In Scripture, earthquakes are associated with God's power and judgment. When the Lord descended to Mount Sinai prior to giving the Ten Commandments, the mountain "was completely in smoke, because the LORD descended upon it in fire. Its smoke ascended like the smoke of a furnace, and the whole mountain quaked greatly. And . . .the blast of the trumpet sounded long and became louder and louder" (Exodus 19:18–19).

When the Lord appeared to Elijah on the same mountain centuries later, there was an earthquake, a powerful wind, a firestorm, and a still small voice (1 Kings 19:11–12).

In the days of King Uzziah, there was an earthquake that came as a rebuke to Judah and Israel (Zechariah 14:5). Psalm 18:7 says, "Then the earth shook and trembled; the foundations of the hills also quaked and were shaken, because He was angry." Job wrote, "He shakes the earth out of its place, and its pillars tremble" (9:6).

Winds come and go seemingly at random. So do waves. Much of the natural world is flexible and transitory—but not the earth itself. Mountains rise and fall over the course of eons, not years or even centuries. What is more stable than rock? What is more grounded than the ground? For these reasons, earthquakes are a specific sign of God's power and the Creator's control over creation. And that sign will increase as we move toward the end of history.

For several years now, scientists have been warning about the possibility of "superquakes," which are earthquakes with incredibly high magnitudes. Believe me, those of us who live in California think about this a lot!

Kenneth Murphy of the Federal Emergency Management Association (FEMA) is deeply concerned about a large-scale earthquake along the Cascadia fault line in the Pacific Northwest of the United States. If this earthquake happened, "FEMA projects that nearly 13,000 people will die in the Cascadia earthquake and tsunami. Another 27,000 will be injured, and the agency expects it will need to provide shelter for a million displaced people."[15]

"This is one time that I'm hoping all the science is wrong, and it won't happen for another thousand years," Murphy said.[16]

Government officials can't predict earthquakes, but Jesus did. He told us the very globe itself would shake as it prepared for His return.

## God's Decrees Are Unconditional

If we're not careful, all this will make us shake as well. But be encouraged by Acts 2:25: "I foresaw the LORD always before my face, for He is at my right hand, that I may not be shaken."

The way to combat the fear of natural disasters is by supernatural discipleship, which allows the Holy Spirit to flood our lives with encouragement, conviction, and hope. Hebrews 6:19 says, "This hope we have as an anchor for the soul, both sure and steadfast, and which enters the Presence behind the veil."

Even in a world defined by disaster, our lives can be defined by confidence. Not in ourselves, of course, but in God. Specifically, there are four elements of God's nature and character that will fill us with confidence as we focus on Him and seek His face.

## Confident in God's Protection

From Genesis to Revelation, God is revealed as someone who watches over His people, keeping them safe in the midst of danger. Throughout the Bible He is described as our Shield, Fortress, Hiding Place, Keeper, Refuge, Rock, Shade, Shelter, and Stronghold.

The Lord told Abram, "Do not be afraid, Abram, for I will protect you, and your reward will be great" (Genesis 15:1 NLT).

The psalmist said, "The LORD is my fortress, protecting me from danger, so why should I tremble?" (27:1 NLT).

Zechariah wrote, "The LORD of Heaven's Armies will protect his people" (9:15 NLT).

Over a hundred years ago, Anna Kay Scott was on a primitive mission field when an earthquake occurred. In her autobiography she wrote:

Sunday, January 10, 1869, we experienced a very severe shock of earthquake. I had just closed my Bible class of young men and was sitting quietly reading letters from the dear home people when I heard the rumbling as of a distant freight train. . . . Soon the house began to rock and the frail bamboo walls to bend. Then there was crash after crash as cupboards, wardrobes and mirrors were thrown down.

Anna rushed from the house to find the villagers standing paralyzed with fear. They were shaking uncontrollably and begging their Hindu gods to stop the elephant. They "believed that the earth stood on the back of an elephant and an earthquake was caused by the shaking of the elephant!"

The quake became so intense everyone fell to the ground. Anna recalled, "The clocks stopped and the river set up-stream for half an hour or more. The earth opened in huge cracks and the yard where we all sat rose in apparent wavelets."

She and the other believers immediately pulled out their Bibles and began reading from Psalm 90: "Lord, You have been our dwelling place in all generations. Before the mountains were brought forth, or ever You had formed the earth and the world, even from everlasting to everlasting, You are God" (vv. 1–2).

The power of those words brought calmness to the village and actually paved the way for more evangelistic work to be done.[17]

The earth doesn't rest on an elephant's back but in the omnipotent hands of the God who tells us, "Since we are receiving a kingdom which cannot be shaken, let us have grace, by which we may serve God acceptably with reverence and godly fear" (Hebrews 12:28).

When we realize the eternal God is our dwelling place and that we're surrounded by His very real, very powerful, and very comforting presence, we are encouraged, and our hearts are full of hope "even though the earth be removed, and though the mountains be carried into the midst of the sea" (Psalm 46:2).

## Confident in God's Pardon

Earlier I made the claim that disasters can produce encouragement and even hope. If that strikes you as unlikely, then I suggest you take a look at a few examples from Scripture that reveal just such a progression.

In the book of Joel, a plague of locusts devastated the land of Judah. Joel used that tragedy as an opportunity to warn people of their sins and turn them toward God.

"'Now, therefore,' says the LORD, 'turn to Me with all your heart, with fasting, with weeping, and with mourning.' So rend your heart, and not your garments; return to the LORD your God, for He is gracious and merciful, slow to anger, and of great kindness. . . . Who knows if He will turn and relent, and leave a blessing behind Him" (2:12–14).

Remember the story of the Philippian jailer? It was an earthquake that brought him to Christ. In great fear, he said, "Sirs, what must I do to be saved?" The apostle Paul said, "Believe on the Lord Jesus Christ, and you will be saved, you and your household" (Acts 16:30–31).

This progression from hurt to hope can still be found in our day. According to Bethany DuVal with TEAM, a global alliance of churches and missionaries, something similar happened to a Mexican woman named Gaby, who had married and had children while very young. She liked the streets and had no interest in her mother's Christian faith. When Hurricane Odile devastated La Paz in 2014, Gaby's makeshift home was obliterated. But a local ministry reached out, provided food, and started helping survivors rebuild their homes.

Soon Gaby found herself helping too, making tortillas alongside a girl named Emily. When Emily invited her to a Bible study, she decided to go. As the two studied Scripture and worked in the kitchen, the Lord dealt with Gaby's heart. Emily later said, "I really got to see how she was giving her life to Jesus . . . and how God was transforming her. . . . We spent many, many days crying in my kitchen and just praying through things."

After she found Christ as Savior, Gaby continued growing spiritually. Today she leads a high school diploma program and works in the kitchen of the same relief agency that reached her with the hope of Christ. "Knowing God and then living in Him is the best gift I have ever received," she said.[18]

That kind of sweet, simple story has been repeated hundreds of thousands of times. I don't understand how it all works, and I don't have all the solutions to the crises we face. But I know that natural disasters bring out supernatural discipleship and that God allows His people to serve those who are hurting even as we share the gospel. In this way, He turns curses into blessings.

Never underestimate how the Lord can use you when difficulty descends on your community or on someone you know.

## Confident in God's Perspective

Geraldine "Gerri" Schappals is a remarkable woman. She survived the Spanish flu as a baby in 1918. She lived through World War II, the Korean War, Vietnam, the Iraq War, and the war in Afghanistan. She survived breast cancer in her sixties and colon cancer in her seventies. In 2020, Gerri contracted COVID-19 at the age of 102—and survived.

"It wasn't bad," she said.

When asked how to stay strong in the middle of difficult times, Gerri said, "One thing that helps is to tell yourself you're not going to fret about it for an hour—it'll still be there at the end of the hour—and go do something enjoyable." She added, "I've found that little breaks can give a fresh perspective and remind you that no matter how dark things are, there are still some little lights."[19]

Fresh perspective is a wonderful gift. And aligning ourselves with God's perspective can produce a huge surge in our confidence. Why? Because His gaze extends from first to last, and He has already told us about the end of our collective story in this world.

For example, near the end of His Olivet Discourse, Jesus said, "As the lightning comes from the east and flashes to the west, so also will the coming of the Son of Man be." He will come "on the clouds of heaven with power and great glory" (Matthew 24:27, 30). Peter told us to be "looking forward to these things" (2 Peter 3:14).

In the final chapter of God's Word, we find another superlative text:

> I heard a loud voice from heaven saying, "Behold, the tabernacle of God is with men, and He will dwell with them, and they shall be His people. God Himself will be with them and be their God. And God will wipe away every tear from their eyes; there shall be no more death, nor sorrow, nor crying. There shall be no more pain, for the former things have passed away." (Revelation 21:3–4)

Not only have we been given this good news, but we are called to share it. Indeed, one of the best ways we can communicate hope during times of disaster is to remind others that such times are temporary. They are fleeting. God's promise of eternal life is grounded on His return and His eternal home for His people—a place where there will be no more death, no more sorrow, no more crying, and no more pain.

What a privilege to offer such a wonderful perspective!

D. A. Carson wrote, "Genuine spirituality cannot live long without an attitude that is homesick for heaven, that lives with eternity's values in view, that eagerly awaits Jesus' return, that anticipates the day when Christ himself will 'bring everything under his control' and 'will transform our lowly bodies so that they will be like his glorious body.'"[20]

Natural disasters reflect the fallen nature of our world; they are evidence of the corruption of sin. Yet it's also true that disasters reflect the temporary nature of this world. Famine, pestilence, earthquakes, and all manner of catastrophes offer concrete proof that God doesn't intend to leave us in this broken place. Even now, He is preparing a perfect home for all who follow Him.

## Confident in God's Provision

Finally, in times of natural disasters, we can find confidence in God's supernatural provision. He has promised to "give us this day our daily bread" (Matthew 6:11).

Do you remember the Old Testament story about the widow of Zarephath in 1 Kings 17? She used her last bit of flour and oil to make bread for Elijah, but from that moment there was always flour in her bin and oil in her jar. God kept her in bread until the famine ended.

Well, Daniil Kiriluk lives in the region of Luhansk, Ukraine, one of the areas hit hardest by Russia's invasion. He's the pastor of a small church made up of his large family and about twenty others.

Pastor Kiriluk and his wife have ten sons and nine daughters. They decided to make bread to share with those affected by the war. In one night, they baked thirty loaves. As people came to get the bread, others brought flour. The more bread they made, the more flour they had.

All the children and grandchildren in the Kiriluk family pitched in, bringing the total number of workers in the home to thirty-three. Even the youngest son helped as he learned how much yeast, flour, and salt to mix. The youngest daughter kneaded the bread. Soon the church was producing 160 loaves per day, and more than a ton of flour was donated.

A ton of bread—and counting!

But it wasn't only bread that was distributed. Gospel newspapers went out with every loaf, and one couple in the church with a distinct gift of evangelism shared the message of Jesus—the Bread of Life. If you were to see the picture of this family lined up by size, girls on one side and boys on the other, you'd praise God for such people whose hope overflows in kindness and evangelism in times of great danger—all aided by God's provision.[21]

I know you've been pinched in recent years. You've felt the pressure of a world on the brink. Even now, we're facing scarcity, inflation, shortages, and financial upheaval. But don't doubt God's ability to provide for you.

The Bible says, "God will provide" (Genesis 22:8).

Paul wrote, "My God shall supply all your need according to His riches in glory by Christ Jesus" (Philippians 4:19).

Of course, such gifts are not intended to benefit you and me alone but to be shared with those in need. Remember these timeless words: "Command those who are rich in this present age not to be haughty, nor to trust in uncertain riches but in the living God, who gives us richly all things to enjoy. Let them do good, that they be rich in good works, ready to give, willing to share, storing up for themselves a good foundation for the time to come, that they may lay hold on eternal life" (1 Timothy 6:17–19).

This is not a time for followers of Jesus to cling to our possessions, grasping what we've earned with tight fingers. Instead, living in a world of disaster gives us the opportunity to open our hearts and open our hands toward those who are struggling—to those who need a boost of hope.

Let us find confidence in God's provision. First, in God's provision for ourselves. God has promised to grant us everything we need, even in times of disaster.

Second, let us build confidence in His provision through us to others. The more God blesses us, the more opportunities we have to extend His provision outward toward others. "God is able to make all grace abound toward you, that you, always having all sufficiency in all things, may have an abundance for every good work" (2 Corinthians 9:8).

People are hungry in the world today, but you and I can feed them. People are sick in the world today, but you and I can minister to them and meet their needs. People have been shaken in the world today, but followers of Christ can offer the encouragement of Christ. We can offer shelter to those who have no shelter. We can support those organizations that are serving displaced and disgraced populations. We can offer hope when life feels hopeless.

In short, you and I have the chance right now to be generous with our resources—and in doing so, to confidently pour out the love of Christ exactly where people need it most. As the author of Hebrews said: "Do not throw away your confidence; it will be richly rewarded" (10:35 NIV).

Speaking of confidence, I want to tell you about a remarkable young man named Jacob Smith. At just twelve years old, Jacob stood atop an 11,000-foot mountain in Big Sky, Montana. He was about to freeride a triple-black-diamond-rated slope. If you're not familiar with that term, freeriding is when a skier tackles a mountain without following a defined path or run. Just a person gliding through the trees and the rocks and the ridges.

Now, a twelve-year-old boy hurtling down professionally rated ski slopes without a trail is impressive enough. But there's something else you need to know about this story that takes it to another level.

Jacob Smith can't see. His vision is technically 20/800, which is four times the level at which a person is declared legally blind.

Nevertheless, on a chilly morning in Big Sky, Montana, Jacob became the first legally blind skier to complete that legendary run. And he hasn't stopped breaking barriers. At fifteen, he is well on his way to becoming a professional in the sport he loves.

How does he do it? Well, Jacob has a secret: his father, Nathan. On every run, Nathan speaks to his son over a two-way radio. When Nathan describes the terrain, Jacob visualizes it in his mind. And when Nathan tells his son to make a turn or to move in a new direction, Jacob obeys. Instantly.

One interviewer asked Jacob how much he trusts his dad.

He answered, "I mean, enough to turn right when he tells me to."

It's this secret weapon—confidence in his father's perspective and his father's direction—that has allowed Jacob to achieve incredible things.

What lesson has he learned from his skiing adventures? "Honestly, no matter what gets thrown in front of you . . . [and] takes you off-guard a little bit, there is always a way to conquer it. To adapt. To make it happen and still do what you wanna do."[22]

As children of God, we have a similar opportunity to navigate the twists and turns of life with confidence, even in the midst of disasters. Why? Because that confidence is based not in our abilities but in the nature and character of our heavenly Father. Not only does He see what's coming in our world, but He has told us in advance how everything will end.

For that reason and that reason alone, you and I can navigate this world of disaster and still *be confident*!

*"The LORD will strengthen him on his bed of illness;*
*You will sustain him on his sickbed" (Psalm 41:3).*

*"God is our refuge and strength, a very present help*
*in trouble. Therefore we will not fear, even though*
*the earth be removed, and though the mountains be*
*carried into the midst of the sea" (Psalm 46:1-2).*

*"Do not worry, saying, 'What shall we eat?' or 'What*
*shall we drink?' or 'What shall we wear?' For after all*
*these things the Gentiles seek. For your heavenly Father*
*knows that you need all these things. But seek first the*
*kingdom of God and His righteousness, and all these*
*things shall be added to you" (Matthew 6:31–33).*

*"Heaven and earth will pass away, but My words*
*will by no means pass away" (Matthew 24:35).*

*"My beloved brethren, be steadfast, immovable, always*
*abounding in the work of the LORD, knowing that your*
*labor is not in vain in the LORD" (1 Corinthians 15:58).*

*"God is able to make all grace abound toward you, that*
*you, always having all sufficiency in all things, may have*
*an abundance for every good work" (2 Corinthians 9:8).*

*"Indeed I have all and abound. I am full, having received from Epaphroditus the things sent from you, a sweet-smelling aroma, an acceptable sacrifice, well pleasing to God. And my God shall supply all your need according to His riches in glory by Christ Jesus" (Philippians 4:18–19).*

*"Since we are receiving a kingdom which cannot be shaken, let us have grace, by which we may serve God acceptably with reverence and godly fear" (Hebrews 12:28).*

*"The prayer of faith will save the sick, and the LORD will raise him up" (James 5:15).*

*"Beloved, I pray that you may prosper in all things and be in health, just as your soul prospers" (3 John v. 2).*

# Chapter 5

# IN A WORLD OF PERSECUTION, *BE PREPARED*

*They will deliver you up to tribulation
and kill you, and you will be hated by
all nations for My name's sake.*
MATTHEW 24:9

Andrew and Norine Brunson were relaxing at a Turkish retreat on the Aegean Sea when the phone rang. "Andrew," said the voice, "the police have just been here looking for you." The call was from the small church Andrew had pastored for twenty-four years in Izmir—the New Testament city of Smyrna, in Turkey.

That was the beginning of a nightmare lasting 735 days. As he later recounted in his memoir, *God's Hostage,* he was kept for a time in a small cell with no chair, nothing but a low bunk, meaning he had

91

to be either standing, walking, or laying on the bed all the time. The toilet didn't flush. His Bible and his glasses were taken away.

Later, Andrew was transferred to Sakran Prison and accused of terror crimes. His cell was filthy—"the floor, the sheets on the bunk bed, the bag of bread covered in thick, green mold . . . the squat toilet covered in human filth."[1]

Pastor Brunson was sometimes housed in overcrowded cells and unable to sleep because of stifling fear and stifling heat. A third of the way into the ordeal, he sobbed to the prison doctor, "I can't handle it. I have constant panic, I don't sleep. I have lost fifty pounds. I have fought for eight months to control myself, and I can't handle it anymore."

More than once, he said, "I was afraid I was going insane."[2]

But the Lord didn't forsake His servant. "Each day I focused on fighting through my fear to reach a place where I surrendered myself to whatever God had ahead for me."[3]

"I had to learn the lesson of Isaiah 50:10," Brunson wrote after his release and return to America. "'Let him who walks in darkness and has no light trust in the name of the Lord and lean on his God.' God was teaching me to stand in the dark, to persevere apart from my feelings, perceptions, and circumstances."[4]

Not long ago, Andrew Brunson spoke again, and his words were sobering. He warned of persecution ahead for the Western church, saying, "I believe the pressures that we're seeing in our country now are going to increase, and one of these pressures is going to be hostility toward people who embrace Jesus Christ and his teaching, who are not ashamed to stand for him. . . . My concern is that we're not ready for this pressure. And not being prepared is very, very dangerous."[5]

I want us to be ready! One of the best ways of preparing is to study the next item in Christ's remarkable list of coming events for the

World of the End: persecution. He said, "You will be handed over to be persecuted and put to death, and you will be hated by all nations because of me" (Matthew 24:9 NIV).

## The Record of Christian Persecution

Persecution against Christians started with the sufferings of Christ Himself—rejected, scourged, crucified, a Man of Sorrows. Then the earliest disciples were arrested, whipped, and forbidden to preach in the name of Jesus, though they would not be silenced. Stephen became the first person to die for his faith in Christ, and the Bible devotes an entire chapter, Acts 7, to that event.

Eleven of the twelve apostles perished violently, all except John, who was banished to the island of Patmos in old age (Revelation 1:9). Peter and Paul died during the reign of Nero, who falsely blamed Christians for the fire that ravaged Rome in AD 64. During that period, Christians were crucified, torn apart by savage dogs, dragged by wild bulls, and burned at the stake to illumine Nero's gardens at night.[6]

From Nero until now, no generation of Christians has escaped the sword or whip, the prisons or dungeons, the tortures, threats, intimidations, and the scorn of the world around them. *Foxe's Book of Martyrs*, published in 1563, is a record of the sufferings of Protestants in England and Scotland. For generations, many Christians kept a copy of this book alongside their Bibles. People didn't want to forget the stories of the heroes of the faith who suffered for Christ. Though filled with gruesome tortures, *Foxe's Book of Martyrs* inspired millions of readers to remain true to the Lord.

The reason the Pilgrims came to America in 1620 was to escape religious oppression—to worship freely and speak the gospel openly.

The First Amendment in the Bill of Rights encompasses religion in the United States.

By now, you might think we'd see a decrease of persecution of people for their personal faith, right? We're no longer living in Roman times or during the Dark Ages.

Think again!

In many parts of the world, the persecution of Christians now exceeds any period in history. According to Dr. Todd M. Johnson of Gordon Conwell Theological Seminary, more than seventy million Christians have been martyred throughout history, and more than half of those deaths occurred in the twentieth century. He also estimates one million Christians were killed between 2001 and 2010, and another 900,000 between 2011 and 2020.[7]

John L. Allen Jr. is one of the most respected journalists in America. In his book *The Global War on Christians*, he wrote, "Christians today indisputably are the most persecuted religious body on the planet, and too often the new martyrs suffer in silence."[8]

## The Reality of Christian Persecution

Each year, the Christian charity organization Open Doors International releases a "World Watch List" highlighting the fifty places where faith in Jesus costs the most. In 2022, Afghanistan, North Korea, Somalia, Libya, and Yemen topped the list. Furthermore, they estimate that 360 million Christians in the world today experience extreme persecution because of their faith. That is one out of every seven believers worldwide.[9]

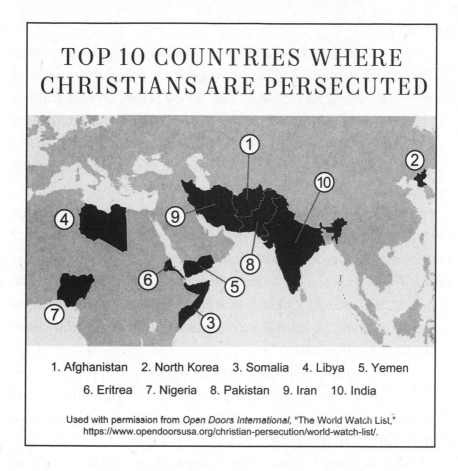

**TOP 10 COUNTRIES WHERE CHRISTIANS ARE PERSECUTED**

1. Afghanistan   2. North Korea   3. Somalia   4. Libya   5. Yemen
6. Eritrea   7. Nigeria   8. Pakistan   9. Iran   10. India

Used with permission from *Open Doors International,* "The World Watch List,"
https://www.opendoorsusa.org/christian-persecution/world-watch-list/.

Jesus foresaw this! Look at Matthew 24:9 again and notice the precision of Christ's words: "They will deliver you up to tribulation and kill you, and you will be hated by all nations for My name's sake."

Each phrase in that prophecy is important. Let's look more closely at the three specific stages Christ predicted: tribulation, death, and hatred.

## Tribulation

First, Jesus foresaw tribulation. The Greek word translated as "tribulation" is *thlipsis*, which describes a grinding pressure or crushing from which there is no escape. Think of how people ground grain in the ancient world. The kernels were pounded and pulverized between two millstones with no chance of relief. That's tribulation.

Jesus said, "In the world you will have tribulation; but be of good cheer, I have overcome the world" (John 16:33).

At this point, Jesus wasn't speaking exclusively about the seven years of intense suffering at the end of the world, the period we often call "the tribulation." He was speaking about the growing buildup of opposition as we move toward those final days. Throughout the future of the church, Christians will experience greater levels of grinding pressure, which will increase in intensity as we grow closer to the World of the End.

As we've learned, all the Matthew 24 signs will reappear after the rapture with greater intensity than ever. That's why the fifth seal of Revelation 6 is persecution and martyrdom. It follows deception, war, famine, and death (vv. 9–11).

But in the buildup toward the rapture, there will be increasing tribulation for God's church. That's where we are now.

For example, the Communist government of China has been tightening the screws on the flourishing Christian movement. The Chinese website Jona Home (as in the prophet Jonah) served readers for more than twenty years by faithfully posting Christian teaching and other helpful content. Then, in April 2022, Jona Home updated its website with a final post: "Due to reasons known to everyone, from now on our site can no longer serve brothers and sisters in Christ. Thanks to all for your company and support in the past 21 years!"[10]

The website had been shut down by the government. The site

administrators were among the first people to experience the effects of a new law established by the Chinese Communist Party (CCP) in March 2022: the Administrative Measures for Internet Religious Information Services. According to that law, any religious group desiring to disseminate information online would need to apply for and receive a special license, available only to religious groups that have already been legally approved by the CCP.

Effectively, the Chinese government has restricted online biblical teaching, curriculum, or devotional content that doesn't "promote socialist values and support the party."[11]

This happened not in AD 22, but in the modern days of 2022— and in a nation with almost 1.5 billion citizens.

The loss of a website may seem of little importance compared to the martyrdom of millions as mentioned earlier. Yet we must understand what's involved with persecution. Enemies of Christ and His church don't always begin with murder and death. Instead, they lay a groundwork of harassment, provocation, and confrontation designed to tyrannize those deemed unacceptable. They label Christians as undesirables. Then, once followers of Jesus have been marginalized, our enemies escalate their efforts toward destruction.

This process is playing out now all over the world. For example:

- In Kaduna state, Nigeria, a group of Fulani herdsmen attacked four villages, killing eighteen Christians and burning down ninety-two houses. The victims were specifically targeted because of their faith in Christ.[12]
- In Eastern Uganda, the head teacher of a private Islamic school converted to Christianity. When teachers heard him praying in Jesus' name, they beat him, scarred him with third-degree burns, and fired him from his position.[13]

- In Vietnam, officials stripped a family of their citizenship after three years of trying to coerce them to stop practicing their Christian faith.[14]
- In Uttar Pradesh, India, a pastor was arrested and tortured by police for twenty-four hours. His crime? Singing out loud to Jesus with his family.[15]
- On the other side of the globe, four Christians in Venezuela were overpowered, beaten, and forced to eat pages from the Bible. Each man was stripped and had a cross slashed across his torso with a knife. The four were workers in a church-run drug rehabilitation center, and their attackers were reportedly members of a drug cartel.[16]

## Martyrdom

In Matthew 24:9 Jesus said, "Then they will . . . kill you." The World of the End will see a dramatic increase in the rise of martyrdom and religious killings—not only in regions of the world dominated by Islam or Hinduism or socialism but everywhere.

The Bible uses the word *martyr* to describe someone who is slain for their faith in Jesus. Acts 22:20 talks about "the blood of Your martyr Stephen." Jesus reminded the church in Pergamos, "Antipas was My faithful martyr, who was killed among you" (Revelation 2:13). Revelation 17:6 speaks of "the blood of the martyrs of Jesus."

In all these examples, the Greek word *martus* was used, which actually means "witness." Throughout the New Testament, we see references to those who witness for Christ by announcing the good news and the facts of the gospel. When these witnesses were killed for their message, the English translators rendered the word as *martyr*.

Kayla Mueller was a modern-day martyr for the cause of Christ. As a Christian, she believed it was her responsibility to join in God's work of relieving suffering in the world. "I find God in the suffering eyes reflected in mine," she once wrote. Addressing God, she added, "If this is how you are revealed to me this is how I will forever seek you."[17]

While serving as a relief worker in Syria, Kayla was taken hostage by members of an ISIS cell. She remained a prisoner for eighteen months, enduring abuse of every kind along with several other female captives. She eventually became a personal prisoner of Abu Bakr al-Baghdadi, the leader of ISIS at the time.

When a group of young women planned to escape their captors, Kayla refused to join them. "I am an American," Kayla explained. "If I escape with you, they will do everything to find us again."[18]

Those young women did escape, and they took with them a letter smuggled from Kayla to her parents. Here's a portion of what that amazing young woman wrote during one of the darkest circumstances imaginable:

> If you could say I have "suffered" at all throughout this whole experience it is only in knowing how much suffering I have put you all through . . . I remember mom always telling me that all in all in the end the only one you really have is God. I have come to a place in this experience where, in every sense of the word, I have surrendered myself to our creator [because] literally there was no [one] else. . . .
>
> By God [and] by your prayers I have felt tenderly cradled in free fall. I have been shown in darkness, light [and] have learned that even in prison, one can be free. I am grateful.[19]

Kayla Mueller was a millennial Christian who died at the hands of Abu Bakr al-Baghdadi. Yet she is victorious today because her story has proven once more the power of light over darkness, freedom over tyranny, and love over hate. Kayla's witness will forever reveal the power of the gospel—a power that endures even in the face of death.

## Hatred

In Matthew 24:9, Jesus also explained *why* we face tribulation and martyrdom. He said, "You will be hated by all nations for My name's sake."

For some twisted reason, the world system has always hated the simple Savior from Galilee. I can't really explain the hostility directed against the greatest man who ever lived and His believers. The true workers of Christ on this planet have done more good than society realizes. Without fear of contradiction, I can say the genuine church of the Lord Jesus has been the greatest humanitarian force in history. Yet for two thousand years, the world has raged against us—seeking to disband the movement Jesus began, ban the Bible He gave, disrupt the ministry He started, and destroy the souls He saved.

Christian persecution at the end of history will not be clinical or detached. It will be fueled by intense emotions. We will be *hated*.

In the past, our ancestors sometimes responded to persecution by fleeing to a new place geographically. The first Christians relocated to Judea, Samaria, and the ends of the earth to escape the fierce backlash of the religious leaders in Jerusalem. Christians fled the wrath of the Roman Empire during the first centuries of the church by pushing ever outward. The Puritans sailed across the ocean to evade persecution and seek religious freedom.

Yet notice what Jesus said in verse 9: "You will be hated by all nations." Escape from persecution will no longer be an option. In the World of the End, there will be no place left to run.

Why? Why must we experience such intense animosity? Look at the last part of verse 9: "You will be hated by all nations *for My name's sake*" (emphasis added). The reason Christians experience persecution now and in the future is because we're aligned with Christ—and the world hates Him.

"If the world hates you," Jesus said, "you know that it hated Me before it hated you. . . . If they persecuted Me, they will also persecute you" (John 15:18, 20).

That raises an important point of clarification regarding this topic of persecution. Many people are mistreated in the world today. Some experience prejudice because of their race or gender or age. Others are mistreated because of their financial class or physical characteristics. Cruelty and vindictiveness are part and parcel of a society corrupted by sin.

Yet when we talk about persecution both now and at the World of the End, we're talking about people who experience harm or harassment specifically because of their belief in Jesus Christ and their connection to His name.

Let me ask you, then: Are you connected to His name? Are you aligned with Him? I'm not asking about your salvation specifically. I'm asking whether you've publicly identified yourself with Jesus Christ in such a way that those who know you also know what you believe.

Here's another way to phrase the question: If your current state or country were to begin actively targeting followers of Christ for persecution, would you be targeted? Or would you slip under the radar because there's little visible difference between your life and the lives of those who do not follow Christ?

These are the kinds of questions we need to consider, and answer, as our culture moves closer to the World of the End. Make no mistake: sooner or later, you and I will need to take a stand.

## The Response to Christian Persecution

How do we do that? Coach Joseph Kennedy has inspired those of us in America with his example. Kennedy watched the movie *Facing the*

*Giants*, in which a struggling football team was uplifted to physical and spiritual success when the coach began praising God.

"I was crying my eyes out," Kennedy said about the film, which he watched while considering a coaching job at Bremerton High School near Seattle. "It was a clear sign that God was calling me to coach. I had never experienced that kind of effect in my entire life. I said, 'I'm all in, God. I will give you the glory after every game right there on the 50 where we fought our battles.'"[20]

As a coach, he would always take a moment to kneel in prayer on the fifty-yard line after the game, win or lose. Sometimes members of his football team joined him for the prayer. Sometimes even players from the other team joined in. But whether in a crowd or alone, Coach Kennedy prayed. After every game. For seven years.

Then in 2015, an opposing coach noticed what Coach Kennedy was doing and reported it to Bremerton High School's principal. Soon after, the school athletic director instructed Kennedy to stop praying after games, citing the school district's policy regarding religious expression.

The coach tried to do as instructed. He skipped his weekly prayer after one game—and immediately regretted his decision. In fact, before he even got home after the game, Kennedy turned his car around, drove back to the empty stadium, and tearfully returned to the fifty-yard line to express his regret to God.

Kennedy resumed his ritual of postgame prayer the following week—and the week after. That's when school officials placed him on leave and then declined to rehire him for the following season. Joseph Kennedy had spent twenty years serving his country as a United States Marine. He was fired for twenty seconds of prayer.

Still, the coach has always been a fighter. He sued the Bremerton School District in 2015, claiming they violated his religious freedoms and constitutional guarantee of religious liberty. Seven years later, in

January 2022, his case was taken up by the United States Supreme Court.

Just as I'm writing this chapter, the news flashed across the internet that in a six-to-three decision, the Supreme Court ruled in the coach's favor!

I just had to shout, "Praise the Lord!"

Whenever possible, we must kindly but bravely stand up for the freedoms that allow for the expression of our faith.

Of course, in some places there is no concept of religious liberty. In those situations, followers of Christ will have to determine the best way to handle specific instances of persecution based on the direction of the Holy Spirit in their individual circumstances. God will guide us.

Still, we can glean several principles from God's Word that empower us in the face of persecution, whenever and however it comes.

## Recount Your Blessings

First, count and recount your blessings! In the Beatitudes in Matthew 5, Jesus said, "Blessed are those who are persecuted for righteousness' sake, for theirs is the kingdom of heaven" (v. 10).

Does that sound confusing to you?

Being persecuted by the world reminds us that we're not part of the world. We're members of God's kingdom. We are children in His family. We can minimize the importance of what we experience in the world because it doesn't matter very much in light of eternity. As the psalmist wrote, "In God I have put my trust; I will not be afraid. What can man do to me?" (56:11).

Todd Nettleton, who has studied persecuted Christians around the world, described what happened to a woman he identified simply as "Sister Tong." She hosted an unregistered church in her home in

China. As a result, she was arrested and sent to prison for six months. Communist authorities tried to "reeducate" her.

Later, when asked about her experience in prison, Sister Tong said, "Oh yes. That was a wonderful time."

Those around her expressed surprise, but she explained that prison was wonderful because God had been there with her in a special way. Nettleton wrote, "It was like He paid extra attention to her during that time, and her heart was warmed daily by His exceptional presence and touch. She felt so close to the Creator of the universe in prison that it was hard to think of that time as anything other than wonderful."

Furthermore, Sister Tong had effectively shared the gospel with many women in prison and had the opportunity to lead several cellmates to Christ.[21]

In some ways, her experience stands in contrast to that of Andrew Brunson, whom I described at the beginning of the chapter. But, as I'll show you, God gave both of them remarkable grace and showers of blessing when they most needed it. The Lord was equally at work in and through both of them.

We all respond differently to the pressures of society, but there's never a time when we can't name our blessings and count them one by one.

## Respond with Worship

That leads to worship! If anyone in history understood the reality of persecution, it was the apostle Paul. From the moment he accepted Christ as his Savior, he was forced to deal with haranguers and harassers who were after his life. He scaled city walls in a basket. He endured beatings and stonings. He was arrested and accused. He was shipwrecked and snakebitten. All because he refused to let go of Christ.

On one occasion, Paul and his partner Silas were beaten with rods and tossed into jail. Acts 16:23 says they were "severely flogged" (NIV). It's impossible to imagine how painful this kind of beating would be. In the classic civil rights book *Twelve Years a Slave*, we read the true story of a man named Solomon Northup who was seized and forced into slavery. He said that when he was being whipped, he thought he would die, that his whole body was on fire.

We assume the rods badly bruised or cut through Paul and Silas's skin, because later the text talks about their wounds. Then the jailer took them into the innermost cell and "fastened their feet in the stocks" (Acts 16:24 NIV).

In that time, stocks were not just for security purposes. They were an additional form of punishment: a square log split in two with holes drilled for the prisoner's ankles. The top half of the log was removed, the prisoner's ankles were positioned in the bottom half of the holes, then the top half of the log was laid down on top of the ankles and fastened. The prisoner might be left in this position for days, seated and unable to move his legs at all.

Sometimes the holes for the legs were stretched far apart to increase the discomfort, and there are examples of the wrists and even the head being immobilized as well.[22]

How did the two men respond? Let's look at the text: "But at midnight Paul and Silas were praying and singing hymns to God, and the prisoners were listening to them" (v. 25).

Here's how R. Kent Hughes explained what at first glance seems baffling: "Paul and his Gospel companions sang because they knew God had called them across the expanse of Asia Minor. They sang because they believed rightly that they were prisoners of Christ and not of Rome."[23]

I agree, but I still can't explain how Paul and Silas could have processed the pain and trauma quickly enough so that by midnight they were singing. Regaining our emotional bearing after that kind of ordeal takes time.

But don't discount the power of worship.

True worshipers of the true God cannot help themselves. They *have* to worship in all the conditions of life. They worship on sunny days and rainy ones. They worship in the palace or in the prison. They worship when uplifted by circumstances, and they worship when all seems lost. Jesus said, "The hour is coming, and now is, when the true worshipers will worship the Father in spirit and truth; for the Father is seeking such to worship Him" (John 4:23).

The people who know their God find healing in worship. They learn to turn their attention from their misery to their Master. It's supernatural. It's of the Holy Spirit!

If we're worshiping God with resolution today, we can worship Him in persecution tomorrow. When we learn to worship God in the noon hour, we'll know to worship Him at midnight.

There's something miraculous in worship. For many years, the persecution of Christians in Northern Nigeria has shocked the world, yet the believers there will not be overcome. One man, Pastor Selchun, was seized by terrorists who cut off his right hand. As it fell to the ground, he raised his remaining hand and began singing, "He is Lord, He is Lord, He is risen from the dead and He is Lord. Every knee shall bow and every tongue confess that Jesus Christ is Lord."[24]

The Lord imparted supernatural grace to that dear pastor at the moment of need, and He will do the same for us in every incident.

So banish shame and sorrow. Let's hold high the gospel in one hand and the cross in the other. The best way to prepare for the coming days is by taking seriously the great opportunities we have for private and public worship. Fill your heart and mind with Scripture and with key songs of the faith.

## Reevaluate Your Suffering

Sometime after his experiences in that Macedonian prison, the apostle Paul wrote these words to the Christians in the city of Rome: "I consider that the sufferings of this present time are not worthy to be compared with the glory which shall be revealed in us" (Romans 8:18).

Suffering and glory—two concepts that seem totally opposed to each other! Yet here they appear as friends. When Paul used the word *consider*, he was indicating something stronger than a mere opinion or expression. In paraphrase, he was saying, "I have decided to consider the sufferings of the world unworthy to compare with the glory that will be revealed. I've thought it through, and that's my biblical view."

Based on his experiences, Paul determined that the sufferings of the present time are a slight thing in comparison with the glory he will experience one day in heaven.

The same is and will be true for you and me. One day in eternity, our sufferings will reveal God's glory because we'll look back at this moment that seemed so terrible, so large, and so unbearable—and we will realize it was nothing in comparison to the wonders of God and all the blessings He has in store for us.

There's one way we can reveal God's glory now, even in the midst of persecution. As I'm sure you've discovered, our world is built on the principles of reciprocity and escalation. If you hurt me, I'm going to hurt you worse. And then I'll expect you to hurt me back, which will give me the green light for even more retribution—and the cycle continues.

As Christians, we reveal God's glory when we break that cycle. We glorify Him when we respond to persecution not with more rage or more vengeance but with the peace of God that passes all understanding.

That's the testimony of a man in Laos known to us simply as Boun. He was imprisoned for his faith. "They put me in stocks," he said, recalling what had happened to Paul and Silas. "The stocks spread my legs apart, and they also put handcuffs on me. . . . They even put smaller [cuffs] on my thumbs. Then they put me in a black room without food for seven days."

For an entire year, Boun was locked in a concrete cell by himself. The only ventilation came from a small rust hole in the metal door. He would put his nose to that hole to breathe. He begged for a Bible but wasn't given one.

During his second year, Boun was given more freedom and permitted to go outside and gather firewood for the camp. When a strong flood brought lots of wood and debris into the camp, the guards let Boun work for hours unnoticed.

One day he saw his chance, swam across the stream, and escaped. He went home, gathered five Bibles, and swam back. The guards never realized he had been gone. He hid four Bibles in the forest and began studying every day and night in his cell. He shared what he was learning with the other prisoners whenever he could.

Six months later, he again escaped and returned, bringing small radios back with him to listen to gospel programming. He gave the Bibles and radios to the other prisoners, and a work of grace began in that prison. One day a guard saw the Bible, and Boun was hauled before the prison authorities who wanted to know what he was studying. Boun opened his Bible and started reading it. After reading a long time, he said, "Oh, I cannot finish it all in one day, but if you want to know more, I will tell you."

The prison warden said, "Your family is so strong in their faith that Christianity has spread everywhere." Shortly afterward, Boun was released. He was overjoyed at his release, but his perception about persecution had changed. He valued His service to God more than His freedom among men.[25]

When we reevaluate what God is doing and why, we realize the sufferings of this present world aren't worth comparing to the opportunities confronting us and the glory awaiting us. The important thing, then, is not what we're going through—but who we're ministering *for* and whom we're ministering *to*.

## Receive Your Reward

Finally, remember what the apostle James wrote about suffering: "My brethren, count it all joy when you fall into various trials, knowing that the testing of your faith produces patience. But let patience have its perfect work, that you may be perfect and complete, lacking nothing" (1:2–4).

Persecution produces the reward of personal growth, the strengthening of our character.

Also remember the historical results of persecution. When the Jewish leaders attacked the leaders of the early church, its members spread across the known world, and God's kingdom grew. When the Romans burned Christians at the stake, the slaves and servants in that empire saw the faithful witness of God's people. They believed, and the kingdom grew. All throughout history, whether in Europe or Africa or China or, yes, even America, the persecution of Christians has again and again fueled the expansion of the church.

Persecution produces the reward of an increasing harvest in God's kingdom. Even at the World of the End, God's kingdom will continue to advance.

In the book of Revelation, Jesus dictated seven letters to seven churches in Asia Minor. One of those churches, Smyrna, was enduring extreme persecution at the time of John's vision. Here is what the Savior had to say to such a church in such a moment:

> These things says the First and the Last, who was dead, and came to life: "I know your works, tribulation, and poverty (but you are rich); and I know the blasphemy of those who say they are Jews and are not, but are a synagogue of Satan. Do not fear any of those things which you are about to suffer. Indeed, the devil is about to throw some of you into prison, that you may be tested, and you will have tribulation ten days. Be faithful until death, and I will give you the crown of life." (Revelation 2:8–10)

As you consider what we will experience as human beings and as the church during the World of the End, I encourage you to remember Jesus' words: "Do not fear any of those things which you are about to suffer." Do not fear harassment. Do not fear the grinding, crushing promise of tribulation. Do not fear even the possibility of suffering and death.

Instead, stand strong. Be firm. Endure. In the words of Jesus, "Be faithful until death, and I will give you the crown of life."

The World of the End will be a place of persecution for God's people, yet we need not be afraid. We have before us Jesus, our Savior, whose wondrous works allow us to face that persecution by recounting our blessings, responding with worship, reevaluating our suffering, and receiving our reward. Persecution is not a time for us to run and hide; it's an opportunity to stand firm and be faithful for our Savior.

For Andrew Brunson, the day finally came when he was placed on trial before a Turkish court that was determined to condemn him. He was terrified, yet he was resolved to remain true to Christ.

After one accusation after another and after a host of false witnesses, the judge asked Brunson if he had anything to say in his defense. By now, the eyes of the world were on him, for his case had garnered global publicity. Brunson stood up, looked the judge in the eye, and said:

> Jesus told his disciples to go into all the world and proclaim the good news of salvation to everyone and make disciples. This is why I came to Turkey—to proclaim this.
>
> There is only one way to God: Jesus.
>
> There is only one way to have our sins forgiven: Jesus.
>
> There is only one way to gain eternal life: Jesus.
>
> There is only one Savior: Jesus. . . .
>
> For the last twenty-five years I have declared Jesus as Savior! For twenty-three years I did it by choice, and the last two years I have been forced to do it from prison, but my message is the same.[26]

The Lord moved the levers of leadership and diplomacy, and Brunson was released to return home to the United States—but he left behind that final word.

Jesus!

In a world of persecution, we must be vigilant, and we must be ready! Don't be anxious about the future; God will give you grace for the moment. Don't be unaware of the dangers; God will turn them into opportunities. The devil cannot win, and the gates of hell will not prevail against the church of Jesus Christ.

Whether we live or die, the gospel is true. Whether we are free or behind bars, our message is the same.

It's Jesus! And Jesus is Lord!

Therefore, in a world of persecution, *be prepared.*

*"Be strong and of good courage, do not fear nor be afraid of them; for the Lord your God, He is the One who goes with you. He will not leave you nor forsake you"* (Deuteronomy 31:6).

*"In God I have put my trust; I will not be afraid. What can man do to me?"* (Psalm 56:11).

*"Be my strong refuge, to which I may resort continually; You have given the commandment to save me, for You are my rock and my fortress"* (Psalm 71:3).

*"Who walks in darkness and has no light: Let him trust in the name of the Lord and rely upon his God"* (Isaiah 50:10).

*"Blessed are those who are persecuted for righteousness' sake, for theirs is the kingdom of heaven"* (Matthew 5:10).

*"What then shall we say to these things? If God is for us, who can be against us?"* (Romans 8:31).

*"'My grace is sufficient for you, for My strength is made perfect in weakness.' . . . Therefore I take pleasure in infirmities, in reproaches, in needs, in persecutions, in distresses, for Christ's sake. For when I am weak, then I am strong"* (2 Corinthians 12:9–10).

*"But even if you should suffer for righteousness' sake, you are blessed. 'And do not be afraid of their threats, nor be troubled.' . . . For it is better, if it is the will of God, to suffer for doing good than for doing evil"* (1 Peter 3:14, 17).

*"If anyone suffers as a Christian, let him not be ashamed, but let him glorify God in this matter"* (1 Peter 4:16).

*"To him who overcomes I will grant to sit with Me on My throne, as I also overcame and sat down with My Father on His throne"* (Revelation 3:21).

# Chapter 6

# IN A WORLD OF BETRAYAL,
# *BE FAITHFUL*

*Many will be offended, will betray one*
*another, and will hate one another.*
MATTHEW 24:10

The man strolling through a public park in Fairfax County, Virginia, didn't look like one of the world's most dangerous spies. He was middle-aged, middle-class, and a bit out of shape. But look more carefully. That plastic bag in his hand? Now you see it. Now you don't.

Robert Hanssen, an FBI agent with top security clearance, had been betraying his country for two decades as a double agent. Starting in 1979, he sold thousands of US classified files to the Russians, including detailed military plans for responding to a nuclear war. He betrayed American operatives, some of whom were executed by the

Russians. He even told the Russians about a secret multimillion dollar eavesdropping tunnel under the Soviet Embassy.[1]

Unknown to Hanssen, the FBI was watching on that day—February 18, 2001—when he made a dead-drop delivery beneath the bridge in Foxstone Park. As they swarmed and cuffed him, Hanssen asked one question: "What took you so long?"[2]

Between 1979 and 2001, Hanssen betrayed his country time and again. The FBI's official statement reveals the depth of his treachery:

> A betrayal of trust by an FBI Agent, who is not only sworn to enforce the law but specifically to help protect our nation's security, is particularly abhorrent. This kind of criminal conduct represents the most traitorous action imaginable against a country governed by the Rule of Law. It also strikes at the heart of everything the FBI represents—the commitment of over 28,000 honest and dedicated men and women in the FBI who work diligently to earn the trust and confidence of the American people every day.[3]

What a bitter phrase: *a betrayal of trust*. A man like Robert Hanssen makes the headlines and history books, but acts of betrayal happen every day in politics, in business, and in life. Perhaps you've been damaged by someone who broke trust with you and, in the process, broke your heart.

What does this have to do with the World of the End? Jesus included *betrayal* in His list of trends that would intensify before His coming. Like all the other items on our list, we're likely to experience this one in greater measure as we move together toward the end of history.

Let's look closer. In Matthew 24:10, Jesus said, "Then many will be offended, will betray one another, and will hate one another."

## The Pain of Betrayal

Few things in life hurt us worse than personal betrayal. If you asked me if anyone has ever betrayed me, I'd answer with a cautious, "Yes." Would you? *Betrayal* is one of the strongest words on the emotional scale. We don't use it lightly. What makes betrayal so raw and painful is that it comes not from our enemies but from those we believed to be our friends. Even our family.

People can't betray us unless we've allowed them through our grid of defenses—unless we've let down our guard and trusted them. Betrayal exposes and exploits our vulnerability. It wounds because it makes us subject to a double-cross. As Les Parrott wrote, "[Backstabbers] put on a front that appears accommodating, loyal, and yes, even sacrificial. Then, without warning, they raise their knife, and by the time you see the glint of the blade, it's almost always too late."[4]

Perhaps you've shared your most private thoughts with someone only to discover they betrayed your confidence and told someone else. Maybe you paid someone in advance for work or equipment without getting what you'd bargained for. Far more painful is discovering your spouse is cheating on you or a sibling has lied to you.

Many people feel betrayed by a dad or mom who failed to love or respect them or by a business partner who did them dirty.

"Honestly, I don't know of any other pain in life that is worse than being betrayed by someone close to you," wrote Phil Waldrep. "It changes everything. After such an experience, the world is simply a different place—one far darker and crueler than you ever thought possible before."[5]

You may be surprised to know "Dear Abby" is still around. This daily newspaper column was started in 1956 by Pauline Phillips, who used the pen name Abigail Van Buren. She chose the name Abigail from the Bible—a "woman of good understanding and beautiful appearance" (1 Samuel 25:3). Abigail gave David good advice, and "Dear Abby" sought to do the same.

Pauline's daughter, Jeanne Phillips, now writes the column. When I come across it, I might skim what's there to see what kind of problems she's dealing with—and if I agree with her advice!

The following letter appeared in "Dear Abby" just as I was working on this chapter, and it's indicative of thousands of problems that have appeared in advice columns over the years.

> DEAR ABBY: Several years ago, my parents betrayed my son and me. They took in and supported my ex-husband, who walked out on us for a coworker he was cheating with. My son and I lost our home, our car, and the life we knew without support from any family. My son was still in high school, and it was a dark time in both our lives.
>
> My parents are both older and have been diagnosed with life-threatening conditions. They are now reaching out to us. To say the least, I am apprehensive. . . . I don't know if I should reconsider a relationship with my parents. Losing my father's support was harder than losing my husband, and I don't want to experience that pain again. Can you advise?
>
> —Burned in Tennessee[6]

How would you have answered? You see, this isn't hypothetical. Every evening, people all over the world go to bed with the feeling they were burned by someone, and the pain lingers for a long time. Many of them seek to forgive and move on, but it's a hard and painful process.

## The Portraits of Betrayal

Let me tell you, there's nothing new about being burned by someone. The sin of betrayal goes back to a cryptic point before the beginning of human history when the archangel Lucifer turned against his Creator. The Lord told him, "I ordained and anointed you as the mighty angelic guardian. You had access to the holy mountain of God" (Ezekiel 28:14 NLT). But this mighty angel deserted his God and led a host of angels in rebellion against Him.

Ever since that point, betrayal has cascaded through the human story like falling dominos.

Adam and Eve were seduced by Satan. Cain betrayed his brother Abel. Jacob double-crossed his brother Esau. Think of how Joseph felt when his own brothers stripped off his colorful robe, threw him in a cistern, and sold him into slavery (Genesis 37:18–36). Delilah betrayed her husband, Samson, and the psalms of David are filled with anguish over various acts of betrayal—including an attempted coup by his own son Absalom.

"It is not an enemy who taunts me," David said on one occasion, "then I could bear it; it is not an adversary who deals insolently with me—then I could hide from him. But it is you, a man, my equal, my companion, my familiar friend" (Psalm 55:12–13 ESV).

There are many more examples of betrayal in the Bible, but only one matches the horrendous betrayal of Satan against God the Father that I mentioned earlier: the betrayal of God the Son by Judas Iscariot. Luke 22:3–4 says, "Satan entered Judas, surnamed Iscariot, who was numbered among the twelve. So he went his way and conferred with the chief priests and captains, how he might betray Him to them."

When we study the character of Judas in the Bible, almost every reference includes his act of betrayal. Matthew introduced him as

"Judas Iscariot, who also betrayed Him" (10:4). Luke described him as "Judas Iscariot who also became a traitor" (Luke 6:16). John said, "And supper being ended, the devil having already put it into the heart of Judas Iscariot, Simon's son, to betray Him" (John 13:2).

Even today, the word *Judas* is a synonym for traitor.

Now put yourself on the Mount of Olives as the sun descends in the western sky. Jesus knew that within hours He would experience the most infamous act of betrayal in history. He must have known that even as He quietly warned those around Him that a spirit of betrayal would engulf civilization as we move closer to the World of the End.

## The Prophecy of Betrayal

That brings us specifically to our next verse in the Olivet Discourse and its three layers of severity—Matthew 24:10: "Then many will be *offended*, will *betray* one another, and will *hate* one another" (emphasis added).

Have you noticed how many of Jesus' prophetic promises in the Olivet Discourse are connected to emotional wounds? Prophecy is about more than earthquakes, pestilence, and heavenly signs. It's also about offenses, betrayal, and hatred.

Every word of Jesus is intentional, so let's trace this trio of terms.

### A World of Offense

The word "offended" in Matthew 24:10 is a translation of the Greek term *skandalizo*, from which we get our modern words *scandal* and *scandalized.* That term is used thirty times in the New Testament, and it refers to a hidden foot-trap in the ground that causes someone to stumble and fall.

I'm sure at some point in your life you've been walking along and didn't see a broken piece of concrete or a root in the ground. It tripped you up and sent you sprawling. That's the picture Jesus painted with the term *skandalizo*. The idea has to do with Satan using other people around us to set traps for us. The Lexham English Bible translates this as, "And then many will be led into sin."

For example, when a Christian engages in some particular habit of sin, he or she tends to take others down the same road. When preachers begin departing from the sound teaching of Scripture, others will be tripped up. When a well-known Christian personality transgresses morally, it causes some to become cynical. When a Christian institution is exposed for ethical failure, it sends some believers stumbling forward, arms flailing in the air. When a preacher, a church, or a denomination begins to minimize a sinful trend in society, it gives weaker believers a license to engage in that sin or even to exalt in it.

That's what it means to trip others up—to be a stumbling block.

Now, there's a vital distinction that is important for us to understand regarding what is often called "the scandal of the cross." Preaching the gospel may offend people who don't want to hear it. As Christians, our biblical worldview may be offensive to those who reject it. I don't want to be personally offensive. Neither do you. Yet regardless of how kindly or lovingly or graciously we teach Scripture, some will be offended by biblical truth.

That is *not* what Jesus was referring to in Matthew 24:10.

To offend someone in the biblical sense of *skandalizo* means to allow spiritual failure to populate in our lives in ways that trip up weaker believers. Jesus warned that this trend would grow and increase leading up to the World of the End. Many will be tripped up and betrayed.

## A World of Betrayal

The Greek word for "betray" is *paradidomi*. It is a relatively common word in the New Testament, used on 121 occasions. That term is translated into several English words, including "deliver," "betray," and "give over." In the context of Matthew 24, it paints the picture of Christians attempting to escape persecution or justify themselves by delivering or handing over other Christians to be judged, punished, or even put to death.

Once again, the saddest part of Matthew 24:10 is the phrase "one another." Christians will betray Christians. Or perhaps more accurately, people who claim to be Christians will betray those who really are.

Earlier I listed some infamous examples of betrayal in the Bible, but there's one more I want to suggest: Alexander the coppersmith. Many commentators believe we first meet this fellow in 1 Timothy 1:20, when he was saying untrue things about God among the churchgoers in Ephesus.[7] Paul removed him from the fellowship of the church, along with another heretic named Hymenaeus. Paul delivered them "to Satan that they may learn not to blaspheme" (1 Timothy 1:20).

What happened next isn't certain, but many commentators believe Alexander harbored a deep bitterness toward Paul and at some point betrayed Paul's whereabouts to Roman authorities. This led to Paul's final arrest, perhaps in Troas. All this took place during the most dangerous days the church had yet experienced, when Emperor Nero declared Christians as public enemies of the Roman government.

If this scenario is correct, Alexander's betrayal led to the imprisonment, trial, and execution of the greatest evangelist and missionary in Christian history. In the final chapter known to be written by Paul, he told Timothy:

Demas has forsaken me, having loved this present world. . . . Only Luke is with me. Get Mark and bring him with you, for he is useful to me for ministry. . . . Bring the cloak that I left with Carpus at Troas when you come—and the books, especially the parchments. Alexander the coppersmith did me much harm. May the Lord repay him according to his works. You also must beware of him, for he has greatly resisted our words. At my first defense no one stood with me, but all forsook me. May it not be charged against them. (2 Timothy 4:10–16)

Do we see current evidence today of Christians being betrayed by family members, neighbors, or even by so-called Christian brothers and sisters? Yes. As we've seen, terrible persecution is afflicting the church in many lands. Intense pressure is sometimes placed on believers to give up the names of other Christians.

Most resist, but some cannot withstand the strain.

Perhaps you know the name Richard Wurmbrand, the author of a widely read book called *Tortured for Christ*. Born into a Romanian Jewish home, Wurmbrand received Christ as his Savior as a young man. During World War II, he preached in bomb shelters and rescued Jews from capture. When the Soviet Union took over after the war, Wurmbrand began working in the Romanian underground church and among underground soldiers in the Russian army.

It was dangerous.

"We had our 'Judases', too," he later wrote, "who told and reported to the secret police. By beating, drugging, threats, and blackmail, the communists tried to find ministers and laymen who would report on their brethren."[8]

Wurmbrand told of a pastor named Florescu who was tortured as authorities tried to compel him to betray his brothers and sisters. The man withstood the pain. Then the officers brought his fourteen-year-old son and began to whip the boy in front of his father. Pastor Florescu couldn't take it and shouted he would tell the police all they wanted to know. But the son shouted, in effect, "Father, don't do it! I don't want to remember my father as a traitor. Withstand it! If I die, I'll be with Jesus."

The boy died praising God, "but our dear brother Florescu was never the same after seeing this," said Wurmbrand.[9]

That sounds like what may happen during the tribulation, when raw evil will operate on steroids. The machinery of the Antichrist will seek to track down all new believers and force from them the names of other converts. But as we've seen, the birth pains are already occurring.

## A World of Hatred

As appalling as betrayal is, hatred is even worse. People may be tricked into betraying you, or they may do so out of weakness. But when people harm out of hatred, they have reached a new level of evil.

Jesus said, "At that time many will turn away from the faith and will betray *and hate* each other" (Matthew 24:10 NIV; emphasis added). This is the second time Jesus has mentioned hate. In verse 9, He warned that the world would hate us, which is a hatred coming from outside the church. But in verse 10, he warned that Christians (or so-called Christians) would "betray one another, and . . . hate one another"—which means Jesus was warning of hatred from within the church.

John Wycliffe understood that type of hate. As an Oxford scholar who loved God's Word, Wycliffe felt a keen burden to help others read and engage with Scripture. But the Bible was only available in Latin during Wycliffe's day, which meant only scholars could read the text. Those scholars then taught the "common people" what they needed to know.

Wycliffe upended this system by spending years of his life translating God's Word from Latin to English. And the church leaders of his day hated him for it.

Here was the church's official position regarding Wycliffe's efforts: "By this translation, the Scriptures have become vulgar, and they are more available to lay, and even to women who can read, than they were to learned scholars, who have a high intelligence. So the pearl of the gospel is scattered and trodden underfoot by swine."

Wycliffe responded: "Englishmen learn Christ's law best in English. Moses heard God's law in his own tongue; so did Christ's apostles."

As the conflict intensified, Pope Gregory XI issued five papal "bulls" (edicts) against Wycliffe with a total of eighteen different charges, labeling the gifted scholar as "the master of errors." Wycliffe was arrested many times, accused of heresy, placed under house arrest, and regularly threatened with death. He died of natural causes before the church could burn him at the stake. However, forty-three years later, church leaders exhumed Wycliffe's corpse, burned the remnants, and scattered the ashes in the River Swift.[10]

That's hatred. And that kind of extreme loathing will become commonplace in the World of the End, even within the established church. Some Christians or fraudulent Christians during that time will fulfill the words of John: "He who hates his brother is in darkness and walks in darkness, and does not know where he is going, because the darkness has blinded his eyes" (1 John 2:11).

We need to realize that genuine followers of Christ—those who are abiding in Christ and growing in Him—are not the sources of hate but the objects of it. Institutionalized religion and apostate Christianity, however, will be vengeful against true believers.

That's why we need to keep all forms of hatred, resentment, and bitterness out of our hearts. It bothers me to see those claiming to follow Jesus harassing other believers over issues of secondary importance. I see Christians verbally abusing other Christians over their political beliefs, their financial expenditures, or their worship styles. Denominational affiliations can cause conflicts. Church fights always cause collateral damage.

Not all of Christ's followers are equally mature. Seasoned Christians should set the model for those who are still babes in Christ. We shouldn't let divisive topics of secondary importance break the bond of fellowship between members of God's kingdom.

## The Preparation for Betrayal

I don't need to convince you that betrayal is painful or persuade you that backstabbing is commonplace in our world. You've seen it. You've felt it.

The real question is, What can we do about it? How do we respond to the reality of betrayal both now and in the future? How do we prepare for it?

The answer: we must be faithful!

Let's think through some steps to take right now as we seek to shine the light of God's goodness and grace into a world struggling with disloyalty.

### Choose Your Friends Carefully

Ashley Garlett grew up in Western Australia, where he and his friends began trying to find ways to have fun. They jumped on and off trains that chugged slowly through their town. They hitched rides on other vehicles too. One night, Ashley and his friend were joyriding on the back of a truck when the vehicle picked up speed. They couldn't get off, and his friend fell to his death.

Ashely was only thirteen, and he dealt with the tragedy by smoking, drinking, and hanging out with a bad crowd of friends. By age nineteen, he realized he was not living the life he wanted to be living.

The answers began to come when he started attending his mother's church. "Eventually I came to know that Jesus died for us," he said. "And he gave his life for us to forgive us our sins. So one day I decided I wanted to respond to the Lord's call and started a new journey for me."

At first, Ashley struggled with how to interact with his old gang. He wanted to share his faith, but he was no longer any fun to them. Even as his old friends rejected him, he began to develop new friends. Now Ashley says, "I want to commit my life to following Christ by helping others come to know him personally and get alongside other brothers and sisters who are passionate and dedicated to serving God."[11]

It's amazing how we're influenced by the friends we choose when we're thirteen—or nineteen, or any other age. How easily we're drawn into unhealthy relationships! Our needs can overcome our judgment, and our feelings can overrule common sense. Before we know it, we're in a relationship that is self-destructive.

In the Bible, Job had a set of friends who came to comfort him in his distress. At first, they wept with him and sat with him in empathetic silence (Job 2:11–13). But when they started giving their opinions and sharing their advice, they upset him until he finally cried out, "Miserable comforters are you all! . . . Have pity on me, have pity on me, O you my friends, for the hand of God has struck me!" (16:2; 19:21).

Despite it all, Job remained loyal to God and to his friends. Even more surprisingly, his friends remained loyal to God and to him. We often rightly criticize Job's friends for their bad advice, but we should remember that at the end of the story they took God's rebuke humbly, offered sacrifices for their sins, and made things right.

"So Eliphaz . . . and Bildad . . . and Zophar . . . went and did as the LORD commanded them. . . . And the LORD restored Job's losses when he prayed for his friends" (42:9–10).

Job's story teaches us many important principles, but this is one of them: friendships may go through ups and downs, but we need friends who will remain loyal to God and to us when all is said and done.

Proverbs 12:26 says, "The righteous should choose his friends carefully, for the way of the wicked leads them astray."

Do your friends help you draw closer to God, or do they push you away from God? That simple question can go a long way toward filling your life with positive relationships.

Another verse in Proverbs says, "A friend loves at all times, and a brother is born for adversity" (17:17). Take a moment to recall a recent time of pain or difficulty in your life. Who was there to help? Who was present with you? And with whom have you stood during their time of struggle?

We need friends who will be honest with us, telling us the truth and keeping us from mistakes or missteps. Proverbs 27:6 says, "Faithful are the wounds of a friend, but the kisses of an enemy are deceitful."

The best way to avoid people who are stumbling blocks or betrayers or hateful is to nurture a handful of rich friendships with people who are sold out to God. If they are loyal to Him, they will be loyal to you. And they will lift you up, not tear you down.

## Stay Focused on Your Purpose

When you find yourself cheated or betrayed in some way—likely despite your efforts to cultivate solid friendships—how should you respond?

Like Jesus.

What did Jesus do when He knew Judas had left the upper room to inform officials of His whereabouts? Jesus still had work to do before

His arrest, and in John 14–16 He gave His disciples the greatest sermon of His life. Then, in the Kidron Valley, Jesus offered His longest prayer recorded in the Bible—John 17.

In the middle of betrayal, Jesus remained focused on His purpose.

Even later, after He was arrested because of Judas's betrayal, Jesus remained steady in the awful work before Him. He didn't let that betrayal derail Him. Instead, He continued forward, even to the cross. The book of Hebrews says that Jesus, "For the joy that was set before Him endured the cross, despising the shame, and has sat down at the right hand of the throne of God" (12:2).

There's a lesson for us. Betrayal can be so painful, so agonizing, that we are unable to focus on anything else. We can't let go. Our hearts become bitter. We chew on the possibility of revenge. All this does nothing except create greater harm.

When you face betrayal, choose to focus not on yourself but on your purpose. Just like Jesus, choose to live above the mindset of bitterness and revenge by pouring your life into the work God has called to you achieve.

I'll say it this way: staying focused on your purpose will allow you to keep the pain in perspective.

## Pursue Loyalty

Walter Orthmann was fifteen years old when he landed his first job. On January 17, 1938, he began working at the Brazilian company Industrias Renaux, which was later renamed ReneauxView.

Would you believe Walter Orthmann is still an employee at that company as I write these words? He started as a shipping assistant and was quickly promoted to sales before shifting to management. He turned one hundred on April 19, 2022. A short time later, he was awarded the Guinness World Record for the longest career in a single company—eighty-four years, nine days, and still counting.

When asked about his record, Orthmann seemed nonplussed. "When we do what we like, we don't see the time go by," he said. "You need to get busy with the present, not the past or the future. Here and now is what counts. So, let's go to work!"[12]

There aren't many Walters around anymore who tackle life with that attitude. Loyalty and commitment are often unpopular because they require us to think of others rather than ourselves. But the beauty in loyalty counterbalances the bitterness of betrayal. We see evidence of that beauty in Scripture:

- "Moreover it is required in stewards that one be found faithful" (1 Corinthians 4:2).
- "But the fruit of the Spirit is love, joy, peace, longsuffering, kindness, goodness, faithfulness" (Galatians 5:22).
- "Do not fear any of those things which you are about to suffer. Indeed, the devil is about to throw some of you into prison, that you may be tested, and you will have tribulation ten days. Be faithful until death, and I will give you the crown of life" (Revelation 2:10).

In a world of betrayal, let us pursue the kind of loyalty that inspires others to remain faithful in their commitment to Christ.

Quintin Campbell entered the US Military Academy at West Point, and he quickly became discouraged. His mother, hearing about it, asked a friend to write Quintin a letter of encouragement. I want to share this letter with you because we could all use the advice.

Cadet Quintin Campbell:

Your good mother tells me you are feeling very badly in your new situation. Allow me to assure you it is a perfect certainty that you will, very soon, feel better—quite happy—if you only stick to

the resolution you have taken to procure a military education. . . .
On the contrary, if you falter, and give up, you will lose the power
of keeping any resolution, and will regret it all your life.

A. Lincoln

June 28, 1862[13]


As with so many other subjects, Abraham Lincoln's advice to that
young man remains helpful today. Don't falter or give up in doing
good and staying true. Keep pressing on without losing the power of
resolution.


## Do Good to Those Who Hate You

We know from Jesus that people will betray us—even people who
call themselves Christians. This *will* happen. We can count on it.
With that in mind, how should we respond?

This is one of those questions to which the Bible gives a simple
answer. We are called to show love and do good to those who harm
us. Even to those who betray us. The Bible couldn't be any clearer on
this matter:

- "If your enemy is hungry, give him bread to eat; and if he is
  thirsty, give him water to drink; for so you will heap coals of fire
  on his head, and the LORD will reward you" (Proverbs 25:21–22).
- "You have heard that it was said, 'You shall love your neighbor
  and hate your enemy.' But I say to you, love your enemies, bless
  those who curse you, do good to those who hate you, and pray
  for those who spitefully use you and persecute you" (Matthew
  5:43–44).
- "Bless those who persecute you; bless and do not curse. . . . Do
  not repay anyone evil for evil. Be careful to do what is right in the
  eyes of everyone. If it is possible, as far as it depends on you, live

at peace with everyone. Do not take revenge, my dear friends, but leave room for God's wrath, for it is written: 'It is mine to avenge; I will repay,' says the Lord" (Romans 12:14, 17–19 NIV).

- "Do not repay evil for evil or reviling for reviling, but on the contrary, bless, for to this you were called, that you may obtain a blessing" (1 Peter 3:9 ESV).

Alfred Lord Tennyson is said to have made this comment about Thomas Cranmer, who was archbishop of Canterbury in the sixteenth century: "To do him a hurt was to beget a kindness from him. His heart was made of such fine soil that if you planted in it the seeds of hate they blossomed love."[14]

You and I carry the same call. Yes, Jesus has warned about the potential of betrayal. But that same Jesus also commanded us to go as far as possible to show goodness and grace. Jesus gave us the Olivet Discourse so we wouldn't be surprised by the hatred around us. He was preparing us to be light in the darkness because that's when the light is all the more impressive and when God looks all the more glorious.

Earlier I wrote about Romanian pastor Richard Wurmbrand. He was himself betrayed by a friend, resulting in fourteen years of imprisonment and torture. Long afterward, a missions leader named Dale Rhoton was walking with Wurmbrand down a street when they saw a man coming their way. Wurmbrand greeted the man with kisses in typical Romanian style, and he introduced the man to Rhoton.

As they walked on, Dale Rhoton said, "Pastor Wurmbrand, that's interesting. The name of that man is the same name as the man who betrayed you."

Without missing a beat, Wurmbrand replied, "Rhoton, we all make mistakes."

Dale Rhoton later said, "If anybody has injured me at all, I need to compare that with what Richard Wurmbrand went through, and I should be able to forgive people pretty easily. . . . He must have been totally convinced of the sovereignty of God."[15]

We're going to need Richard Wurmbrand's attitude and his grip on God's sovereignty because the World of the End means increasing betrayal.

### Count on the Character of God

And that brings me to my final suggestion: In the midst of betrayal, count on the character of God. Grasp the sovereignty of God. Lean on the love of God.

This was the conclusion Joseph made after years of processing his brothers' betrayal. He said, "Do not be afraid, for am I in the place of God? But as for you, you meant evil against me; but God meant it for good, in order to bring it about as it is this day, to save many people alive" (Genesis 50:19–20).

When Paul was sold out by Alexander the coppersmith, he pressed on to write his final book, 2 Timothy, with the resolution of finishing his race and keeping the faith. That final epistle contains these words: "But the Lord stood with me and strengthened me, so that the message might be preached fully through me, and that all the Gentiles might hear. Also I was delivered out of the mouth of the lion. And the Lord will deliver me from every evil work and preserve me for His heavenly kingdom. To Him be glory forever and ever. Amen!" (4:17–18).

Perhaps the key to processing the betrayal we experience as followers of Jesus is reckoning that for every person who deserts us, God has blessed us abundantly more with His never-ceasing faithfulness.

Friends will fail us and foes assail us, but our Savior will never leave us or forsake us. His loyalty is as immeasurable as His love. His overruling sovereignty will eventually turn our moments of bitterness into occasions for praise. Count on it!

The apostle Paul said, "I am persuaded that neither death nor life, nor angels nor principalities nor powers, nor things present nor things to come, nor height nor depth, nor any other created thing, shall be able to separate us from the love of God which is in Christ Jesus our Lord" (Romans 8:38–39).

## Faithful to The End

In 1850, John Gray arrived with his family in the city of Edinburgh, Scotland. Though he was a gardener by trade, there was a shortage of work in the city. So John joined the Edinburgh police force as a night watchman. Every evening, he walked the streets to ensure their safety.

John Gray did not walk alone, however. His constant companion was a little Skye terrier named Bobby. No matter the temperature or the weather outside, John and Bobby could be seen walking together through the streets at night, alert for any trouble or any cry for help.

After many years of performing his job with dedication, John died from tuberculosis. He was buried in a cemetery called Greyfriars Kirkyard within the city.

Bobby the terrier refused to leave his master's side. Every day he came to spend long hours lying by John's grave. At first, the kirkyard gardener attempted to shoo the dog away. But after months of witnessing Bobby's faithfulness, the gardener made a small shelter so the little dog could be out of the weather while continuing his silent vigil.

The dog was later nicknamed Greyfriars Bobby, and he visited his master's grave every day *for fourteen years* until he also passed away. The residents of Edinburgh erected a granite fountain outside the cemetery with a statue of Bobby on the top. You can still read his headstone today: "Greyfriars Bobby—died 14th January 1872—aged 16 years—Let his loyalty and devotion be a lesson to us all."[16]

Yes, let's learn the value of loyalty in an age of treachery. Let it always be said that followers of Jesus are faithful and true—even in a world of betrayal such as the World of the End.

Don't let such a world trip you up or drag you down. Instead, *be faithful.*

*"Know that the LORD your God, He is God, the faithful God who keeps covenant and mercy for a thousand generations with those who love Him and keep His commandments"* (Deuteronomy 7:9).

*"Let your heart therefore be loyal to the LORD our God, to walk in His statutes and keep His commandments, as at this day"* (1 Kings 8:61).

*"The eyes of the LORD run to and fro throughout the whole earth, to show Himself strong on behalf of those whose heart is loyal to Him"* (2 Chronicles 16:9).

*"Let not mercy and truth forsake you; bind them around your neck, write them on the tablet of your heart, and so find favor and high esteem in the sight of God and man"* (Proverbs 3:3–4).

*"The righteous choose their friends carefully"* (Proverbs 12:26 NIV).

*"A friend loves at all times, and a brother is born for adversity"* (Proverbs 17:17).

*"If your enemy is hungry, give him bread to eat; and if he is thirsty, give him water to drink; for so you will heap coals of fire on his head, and the LORD will reward you"* (Proverbs 25:21-22).

*"If we are faithless, He remains faithful; He cannot deny Himself" (2 Timothy 2:13).*

*"The LORD will deliver me from every evil work and preserve me for His heavenly kingdom" (2 Timothy 4:18).*

*"Do not fear any of those things which you are about to suffer. Indeed, the devil is about to throw some of you into prison, that you may be tested, and you will have tribulation ten days. Be faithful until death, and I will give you the crown of life" (Revelation 2:10).*

# Chapter 7

# IN A WORLD OF LAWLESSNESS,

# *BE KIND*

*Because lawlessness will abound, the*
*love of many will grow cold.*
MATTHEW 24:12

Zaki Anwari was seventeen, good-looking, athletic, and a rising star on Afghanistan's national soccer team. He spent hours practicing each day, trying to emulate his hero, Argentinian footballer Lionel Messi. "He couldn't get enough," said Zaki's older brother. "It was all he talked about, all he did."

Zaki was born after September 11, 2001. He didn't remember the brutal rule of the Taliban or the early chaos of the war in Afghanistan. He grew up in Kabul in relative peace and prosperity, thanks to the presence of American forces.

When President Joe Biden announced he would withdraw US troops from Afghanistan in August 2021, Zaki felt apprehensive. He had heard reports of Taliban forces heading toward Kabul. As the Afghan resistance collapsed, Zaki feared for his family and his future. Most of all, he grieved the loss of becoming a soccer star. The Taliban banned most sports, instead rounding up young men and forcing them to participate in Islamic religious rituals and live under strict control.

On August 16, Zaki went to Kabul International Airport with his older brother and a cousin who had worked for an American company to attempt to secure passage out of Afghanistan. There had already been one suicide bombing in the city, and the people were beginning to feel panicked. Taliban forces were close, nearly surrounding the city. The US-backed government was showing more and more signs of imminent collapse.

The plan was for Zaki to watch the car while the older men negotiated. But Zaki jumped the fence and entered the airport.

It's not clear what happened next. At some point, Zaki made his way onto the tarmac as a US Air Force C-17 prepared to take off. He ran toward the plane and raced alongside the aircraft. As the plane accelerated to 120 miles per hour, he was knocked off balance and fell under the wheel. Among his final known words were: "Pray for me. I am going to America!"[1]

Why would anyone run alongside an airplane as it took off? Desperation. Rising terror in the heart. Lawlessness. Violence. Chaos. Brutality.

Any of those answers will do, and all of them increasingly describe our world. We see it most vividly in today's failed states such as Yemen, Somalia, Syria, and, yes, Afghanistan, where law and order have collapsed. Extremists fill the void, fomenting hatred and exporting terror.

It's difficult for you and me to understand the gruesome life that befalls a people when atrocities reign and leadership comes from thugs. Most of us in America and the West have felt relatively safe. We elect leaders who swear to uphold the law. We have law enforcement agencies and emergency response systems populated by millions of good and decent people.

But something is changing. Our police officers have been so vilified by the media they're finding it hard to do their jobs. Politicians curb law-enforcement budgets and prosecutors release those arrested. With open borders, it's difficult to control human smugglers, sex traffickers, and dangerous drugs. Our Western nations have become so divided we never know when an incident will provoke rioting in our streets and violence in our neighborhoods.

What's happening to us?

The answer is just what Jesus predicted in the Olivet Discourse: "Because lawlessness will abound, the love of many will grow cold" (Matthew 24:12).

## Life in a Lawless World

Let's review the sequence of events that will take place before the rapture of the church—remembering the birth-pains principle that these same events will continue to accelerate in frequency and intensity during the tribulation.

Deceivers will come. Wars and rumors of wars will rage. Famines, plagues, and earthquakes will increase in size and scope. The world authorities will track down Christians, with persecution spreading to all corners of the globe. We'll face betrayal and hatred, and many false prophets will rise up and deceive multitudes.

With this cascading torrent of crises, it's not surprising to learn that violence will increase and love will proportionally decrease.

Yet there's an even deeper reality behind these trends. They represent a collective rejection of Jesus Christ on this planet. This is the fulfillment of Psalm 2, which is quoted seven times in the New Testament, including in the book of Revelation.

> Why do the nations conspire and the peoples plot in vain? The kings of the earth rise up and the rulers band together against the LORD and against His anointed, saying, "Let us break their chains and throw off their shackles." (vv. 1–3 NIV)

Everything Jesus described in His Olivet Discourse will create distance between humanity and heaven. Nations will intentionally abandon the values and priorities prescribed in Scripture. Cultures will uncouple from institutions that provide the safety, security, and success we currently take for granted.

Dietrich Bonhoeffer put it this way: "The most experienced psychologist . . . knows infinitely less of the human heart than the simplest Christian who lives beneath the cross of Jesus. The greatest psychological insight, ability, and experience cannot grasp this one thing: what sin is."

Bonhoeffer went on to say, "Worldly wisdom knows what distress and weakness and failure are, but it does not know the godlessness of man. And so it also does not know that man is destroyed only by his sin and can be healed only by forgiveness. Only the Christian knows this."[2]

Jesus knew that! Look again at Matthew 24:12: "*Because* lawlessness will abound, the love of many will grow cold" (emphasis added). The word *because* implies a cause-and-effect relationship between the two clauses of that sentence. As people reject the justice that comes from God's righteousness, they will forfeit the love that comes from His grace. This, then, becomes a vicious downward cycle. Lawlessness begets lovelessness, and lovelessness produces more lawlessness.

## Wickedness Will Increase

When Jesus said, "Lawlessness will abound," He was describing more than the absence of laws or law enforcement. His words call to mind periods of human history that were defined by chaos and disorder—the Dark Ages, for example, or the bloody legacy of the first half of the twentieth century. Or, as I said earlier, today's failed states and terrorist havens. But the lawlessness Jesus pointed to at the World of the End will be exponentially worse than anything we've witnessed before.

Biblical scholar Frederick Dale Bruner describes this future period as a season of "unique lawlessness" in which the very concept of morality will be turned upside down. Right and wrong will be inverted, with entire cultures celebrating what is evil and condemning what is good.

In Bruner's words, "Sinful human beings always practice lawlessness, but there will be a unique lawlessness at the end. Good will be called evil and evil will be called good on a massive and unprecedented scale, exponentially. People will 'glory in their shame.'"[3]

The prophet Isaiah offered a foreshadowing of this season of lawlessness: "Woe to those who call evil good, and good evil; who put darkness for light, and light for darkness; who put bitter for sweet, and sweet for bitter! Woe to those who are wise in their own eyes, and prudent in their own sight!" (Isaiah 5:20–21).

John Staddon has witnessed this unique inversion of right and wrong. As a distinguished professor of psychology and neuroscience at Duke University, he has authored six books and written more than two hundred scholarly research papers. He is well regarded as an expert in multiple fields of study.

Yet Staddon was recently expelled from a psychology and neuroscience forum sponsored by the American Psychological Association. The reason? Staddon spoke openly in the forum about the biological reality of two sexes: male and female.[4]

We see the same twisted logic in other headlines:

- The United States Department of Justice recently equated parents as "domestic terrorists" for pushing back against school boards and other groups teaching children to judge people on the color of their skin rather than the content of their character.[5]
- In Kenosha, Wisconsin, violent protestors were celebrated as heroes after setting buildings on fire and looting businesses. Local firefighters responded to thirty-seven separate fires during a single night of protesting.[6]

Abortion is the most extreme example of immorality being celebrated as morality. Since the landmark Supreme Court decision known as *Roe v. Wade*, there have been more than 63 million abortions carried out in the United States alone. That means there are 63 million human beings, created in the image of God, who were legally and officially denied the right to exist.

Thankfully, the Supreme Court has struck down the legal precedent of *Roe v. Wade*, ending the federal protection of abortion as a constitutional right. I watched the reaction to that ruling with interest. The rage of the pro-choice advocates exposed the vehemence with which they disregard the most basic of all civil rights—the right to live.

While society is moving ever closer to the World of the End, we feel the currents of the tribulation blowing backward into our own atmosphere. As never before, we need to be able to articulate biblical positions on moral issues without confusing or reversing right and wrong.

And, as never before, we need to understand that the growing insanity in our world isn't primarily a political or military problem. It is a spiritual problem. The further our world strays from Christ, the closer it drifts toward cruelty and chaos. Jesus said wickedness will increase.

## Love Will Grow Cold

This growing wickedness will cause the love of many to grow cold. The New International Version of Matthew 24:12 says, "the love of most will grow cold." Not just *many* people, but *most* people! The further we drift from God's justice, the less we will reflect God's love, and the more anger will beget anger.

Years ago, I remember seeing a cartoon showing four panels. In the first, a boss was chewing out an employee. In the next, the employee was coming home and snapping at his wife. The third panel showed the wife chewing out the young son. And in the last panel, the boy was kicking the dog.

Anger produces a chain reaction that can travel around the globe, and it can do it now with the click of a button. We never know where violence will erupt next.

While working on this chapter on the Fourth of July, I took a moment to check the headlines. A gunman started shooting at an Independence Day parade in Highland Park outside Chicago. At least seven people were killed and dozens wounded as he fired away from a rooftop perch with a high-powered rifle. Initial reports indicated he had been planning the attack for weeks!

The mayor of Highland Park actually knew the alleged gunman from many years earlier when he participated in the Boy Scouts. Her statement feels all too familiar: "It breaks my heart," she said. "I see this picture and through the tattoos, I see the little boy. I don't know what got him to this point."[7]

What indeed? Pundits debate the reasons for these kinds of things—guns, mental illness, broken homes, drugs. All those things may play a part, but the root cause that got all of us "to this point" is identified in Matthew 24:12. Because of the increase of violence, true godly love as a human force is being frozen out of our culture, which in turn begets more violence.

Because of growing wickedness, the love of most people "will grow cold." That phrase is a translation of the Greek root word *psycho*, which literally means "to breathe or blow." That's where we get our English words *psyche* and *psychology*.

But in Matthew 24:12, the word is used literally in the sense of blowing air across something. Think of your coffee when it's too hot to drink. What do you do? You blow on it, allowing the air to stir the top of the liquid, cooling it just a bit. That's the word picture Matthew used. As the winds of lawlessness blow across our world, it chills our love, and the world becomes a colder place.

Need more evidence? Think of the loneliness and lostness of multitudes of people around us. A recent study concluded that 36 percent of all Americans experience "serious loneliness" in a way that significantly impacts their lives. This includes a whopping 61 percent of young adults.[8]

Look also at the rise in "diseases of despair" over recent decades, including addiction, anxiety, depression, suicide, and more—all of which are skyrocketing in America and across the world. In fact, the medical journal *BMJ* recently conducted a review of health insurance claims between 2009 and 2018. Scholars found a 68 percent increase in diseases of despair on a broad level during that time span:

- Suicidal thoughts and behaviors among children (those under 18) increased by 287 percent over that ten-year span.
- The rate of substance abuse recorded within adults aged 55–74 increased by 172 percent.
- Substance abuse among infants rose by 114 percent, which is directly related to addictions among young mothers.

# DISEASES OF DESPAIR
# BETWEEN 2009-2018

**Suicidal thoughts and behaviors** among children (those under 18) increased by **287%**.

The rate of **substance abuse** recorded within adults aged 55–74 increased by **172%**.

**Substance abuse** among infants rose by **114%**, which is directly related to addictions among young mothers.

According to the study, "Diseases of despair diagnoses were associated with significantly higher scores for coexisting conditions, higher rates of anxiety and mood disorders, and schizophrenia for both men and women across all age groups."[9]

Remember, all that was before COVID-19. Love is draining away from our world, and that trend will only accelerate as we move closer and closer to the end of history.

## The Way of Kindness

It's difficult to watch the world disconnect from God. Humanity's slide toward lawlessness and lovelessness is painful. We feel a jolt when outside forces corrupt the institutions and customs we've cherished for so long. The darkness seems to be deepening over our culture like the edge of night.

But we are not powerless. We are "children of God without fault in the midst of a crooked and perverse generation among whom [we] shine as lights in the world, holding fast the word of life" (Philippians 2:15–16).

As for me, I'm not willing to sit passively as humanity turns its back on God's justice and God's kindness. Yes, the trends are going in the wrong direction as we approach the World of the End, but the church is still on earth, and we can still make a difference!

One of the biggest ways we can make a difference is by bringing back a revolutionary concept called kindness, which in many ways is the antidote to lawlessness. We have limited ability to control the lawlessness and lovelessness in our society—but we can control how we respond to those factors. Specifically, we can use those realities as opportunities to offer kindness even when others don't deserve it—in fact, especially when they don't deserve it!

As I've pondered this, I've jotted down for myself three specific ways I can show kindness in a culture of wickedness, and I'd love for you to join me.

## Embrace God's Kindness

Before we can demonstrate God's love and kindness to anyone in the world, we need to embrace that love and kindness for ourselves. Rich Mullins wrote his best-known worship song, "Awesome God," in 1988, and he sadly died in a highway accident in 1997. A few years later, James Bryan Smith wrote a book about Rich's life, in which he shared how Rich grieved that his dad never spoke the words, "I love you."

Rich also battled feelings of worthlessness as a teenager. "God," he once prayed, "Why am I such a freak? . . . I wanted to be a jock or something. Instead I'm a musician. I feel like such a sissy all the time. Why couldn't I be just like a regular guy?"[10]

Despite his struggles, Rich attended church, read his Bible, and began writing worship songs. Along the way he truly began to embrace the love of God. It struck him when he looked at the creation around him. He became awed that God, in His love, gave songs to the birds, majesty to the mountains, and laughter to the children—all for our benefit.

Rich became centered on Jesus. Rich's brother, David, said that Rich "always struggled with feelings of self-worth. But he found his worthiness in Christ's death for Him."

Rich once told a concert crowd, "If you only knew how crazy about you God was! God has already loved you, if only you knew!"[11]

Rich's mother, Neva, later said, "He actually felt God's love. I think because he was a stranger everywhere he went, he leaned into God and drew close to Him. He was not a saint, but it was his sense of being loved by God that made him different."[12]

Rich's biographer said, "Rich discovered that the love God has for us is not an emotion but it is in fact the essence of who God is. The death of Christ is the indisputable sign . . . that shouts to us, 'God loves you! God loves you!'"[13]

I know many people reading these words have been jolted by life. Like Rich Mullins, you've not had the human love you needed. Perhaps you've been abused, neglected, or mistreated. We all battle issues of self-worth, and perhaps everyone wonders at some point whether God loves them. You may feel all alone.

If only you knew how crazy God is about you! He really loves you! It's our being loved by God that makes us different, and His love isn't mere emotion. It's the essence of who He is.

Oh, may God give you "power, together with all the Lord's holy people, to grasp how wide and long and high and deep is the love of Christ, and to know this love that surpasses knowledge—that you may be filled to the measure of all the fullness of God" (Ephesians 3:18–19 NIV).

People who possess that knowledge are insulated from the chilling winds that cause warm love to become hard ice. When we embrace the love of God through Christ, our own love will not grow cold.

That's why Paul reminded the earliest believers, "The love of God has been poured out in our hearts by the Holy Spirit who was given to us" (Romans 5:5). And that's why John said, "We love because he first loved us" (1 John 4:19 NIV).

On a practical level, our sense of God's love deepens as we spend time with Him. I've experienced many wonderful things throughout my decades of serving God. But the foundation for those experiences is nothing more complicated than my daily quiet time in His presence. I'm talking about prayer. I'm talking about studying His Word. I'm talking about worship that is both public and private. These are the ways that keep the love of God simmering in our hearts.

It's very hard for your love to grow cold when the fervent love of God is surging through your veins.

## Express God's Kindness

When we embrace God's love, it becomes natural to express His love. In many ways, kindness is God's love expressed through action. And nothing is more obvious in the Bible than God's commands to love this world in tangible ways, such as providing a "cup of cold water" in Jesus' name to the thirsty (Matthew 10:42).

The leaders of Bear Creek Community Church in Lodi, California, took on that very task. They felt a burden to help provide safe water to impoverished parts of the world. The project wasn't in the church's budget, and many of the congregation's families were already under financial strain. Who took up the challenge, then? The children's ministry!

There's a strong recycling emphasis in California, and the children began collecting bottles and cans to bring with them to church.

Other congregations rallied to the cause, and would you believe it—so far they have raised nearly a million dollars for clean water projects around the world!

Dr. Michael J. Mantel described this wonderful news by saying, "Jesus turned water into wine. The kids at Bear Creek turned garbage into water."[14]

This isn't a call for a select few followers of Jesus but all Christians. The Bible says, "Defend the poor and fatherless; do justice to the afflicted and needy" (Psalm 82:3).

And Proverbs 14:21 says, "Blessed is the one who is kind to the needy" (NIV).

Jesus said, "He who has two tunics, let him give to him who has none; and he who has food, let him do likewise" (Luke 3:11).

James said, "Pure and undefiled religion before God and the Father is this: to visit orphans and widows in their trouble" (1:27).

The apostle John said, "But whoever has this world's goods, and sees his brother in need, and shuts up his heart from him, how does the love of God abide in him?" (1 John 3:17).

Expressing God's kindness means fulfilling these commands in small ways such as raking our neighbor's yard or giving a very generous tip to a server in need. We can also reflect God's kindness in large ways such as taking care of an aging parent or helping a friend walk through an addiction. And of course, there is a whole range of options in the middle.

The point is that we *do* something. God's love is not about warm thoughts or well-wishes. It is expressed through action. Through actually being kind.

In expressing God's love through our daily attitudes and actions, we'll keep it boiling. We'll keep it fervent. It's hard for the devil to blow his cold breath over a heart percolating with God's love for those in need.

Here's something else to consider: sometimes the ones with the greatest needs are those closest to us.

Mary Daniels had to face the hard truth that her husband, Steve, was afflicted with Alzheimer's disease. She made him a simple promise: he would never be alone. She would always care for him.

Mary was faithful in her promise for seven years. She stayed by Steve's side even when his condition worsened and he was transferred to a long-term care facility. Every evening, Mary sat next to Steve and watched a familiar sequence of TV shows to help him wind down his day: the local news at six, then *Judge Judy* at seven, followed by *Family Feud* at seven thirty. Then Steve would drift off to sleep.

But when COVID-19 came, assisted-living facilities were closed to visitors. FaceTime conversations proved unhelpful because of Steve's limitations with technology. When Mary attempted to see and comfort her husband through a windowpane, he only sobbed in misery at not being able to hold her hand.

Mary's solution? She took a part-time position as a dishwasher at Steve's facility. She worked her first shift on July 3, 2020. Having logged five hours washing cups, plates, pans, and silverware, Mary was allowed to don a blue surgical gown and walk the familiar steps to her husband's room, where they resumed their comforting routine.

But Mary's fight wasn't finished. She knew many vulnerable residents were in desperate need. Mary began to share her story, which went viral. She was appointed by Florida governor Ron DeSantis to a seven-person task force designed to reunite families safely during the pandemic. Later she joined a federal task force to create the Essential Caregivers Act to make sure family members are not separated again during a public health emergency.

"I don't know that I've seen a singular person that had that much impact in a long time," said US representative John Rutherford of

Jacksonville, Florida. "You've got to have that champion who will pick up the flag, and they're going to carry that flag, and they're going to fight for that cause and not let it go. And that was Mary."[15]

That's the spirit I'm recommending for you and me as we contemplate the darkness and wickedness of the World of the End. Those of us who know God and have embraced His love must resist the urge to grow callous or complacent. We must carry the flag of Christ. We must embody His kindness and share it with others in tangible ways that meet real needs in today's world.

## Embody God's Kindness

How do we pour out kindess in a world increasingly defined by lawlessness? First, by embracing God's love daily so it fills us up. Second, by intentionally expressing that love to others through regular action. Third, as we encounter God's love in greater degrees—both receiving and giving—we will begin to embody that love. Meaning, God's love will become part of our identity.

Let me say this as simply as I can: there is no better solution to the World of the End than for God's people to embody God's kindness to a world in need.

A young man named Hunter Shamatt caught a glimpse of that solution after he flew to Las Vegas for his sister's wedding. When he arrived at the hotel, he realized he'd lost his wallet. More than that, he'd lost the $60 cash, $400 signed paycheck, ID, and bank card that were inside his wallet. The young man tried to maintain a brave face throughout the festivities celebrating his sister, but he was devastated. He needed that money.

Then, to his very great surprise, Hunter received a package the day after he returned home. Inside was his wallet. And inside the wallet was his bank card, ID, $400 signed paycheck—and not $60 cash, but $100! There was also a note that read:

Hunter, found this on a Frontier flight from Omaha to Denver—row 12, seat F wedged between the seat and wall. Thought you might want it back. All the best.

P.S. I rounded your cash up to an even $100 so you could celebrate getting your wallet back. Have fun!!!

Having read the note several times, Hunter was dumbfounded. "No way," he kept saying. "That can't be. Just no way."[16]

That's a mundane story when compared with the grand scope of history, but it offers a picture of what I mean by embodying God's love. What if you and I were to reflect God's love to such a degree that the world around us felt astounded? Even dumbfounded? What if we were to offer God's love with such generosity and such regularity that people said, "No way. That can't be"? What kind of difference could we make if we achieved that level of goodness and kindness in a world afflicted on every side by wickedness?

Jesus gave us another picture of what it means to embody God's love, and I want to introduce it by walking you through a little exercise. Take a moment to transport yourself mentally back to the ancient world of Jesus' day. It's late in the evening. The sun has set, and the last of its light is fading from the night sky. You've been walking for more than ten hours under the heat of that sun, and you're not sorry to see it go. But you're also tired. And sore. And hungry.

Then you see it: a glimmering light in the distance. After another few minutes of walking, that light becomes the welcoming glow of a city built next to the road on the side of a hill. The light you see is not produced by wires and bulbs but by cookfires and hearths and oil lamps hanging on doorposts. There are people in that city. And water to wash the grime off your feet. And a table to recline by as you take your evening meal.

As a weary traveler, can you imagine anything warmer and more wonderful in that moment? Could you stumble upon anything more welcoming and refreshing?

That is the image Jesus used to describe how His church should shine the light of the gospel in the middle of a dark and dreary world: "You are the light of the world. A city that is set on a hill cannot be hidden. Nor do they light a lamp and put it under a basket, but on a lampstand, and it gives light to all who are in the house. Let your light so shine before men, that they may see your good works and glorify your Father in heaven" (Matthew 5:14–16).

Here's a simple principle: light shines brightest in the darkness. And in a world frozen from lawlessness and the lack of love, you and I have the opportunity to radiate the radical warmth of the gospel. The warmth of community. The warmth of kindness. The warmth of fellowship. The warmth of intimacy with our Creator.

Though we have limited control over the overall trends of lawlessness and lovelessness in our culture, we can control how we respond personally to those realities. We can choose to display forgiveness rather than bitterness. We can choose to heal rather than harm—to help rather than hurt. We can choose to be welcoming witnesses when everyone else practices the emotional equivalent of social distancing.

In short, we can be kind.

## Jesus Makes the Difference

It's true that our world has lost something important. We've drifted away from God's justice and love. Not just drifted—we've defected. Humanity is in the process of intentionally rejecting its Creator, and the future may feel bleak.

But you and I have an opportunity to capitalize on those losses. We can show the world what's missing. We can take a stand for goodness and kindness and return what's been lost, even if only for a season. As we do so, we can add that little extra gift that makes all the difference—an extra serving of God's love.

Let me give you one final example of how Jesus alone can deal with the lawlessness and lovelessness of our society.

Budi Mulyadi grew up in Southeast Asia. When he was thirteen, he got into a violent argument with his father and ran away from home. Soon he was placed in an Islamic boarding school, but the rules were very strict. Budi ran away again.

That's when he met an Islamic extremist who promised him a new life. The man took Budi to a large training compound where, with about twenty other boys, he slept in tents at night and trained with knives and guns during the day. These boys were taught to hate and to kill Christians.

"We were told that Christians were infidels," Budi said. "If we would kill Christians, then that would be a free ticket to heaven for us."

The more Budi trained, the more hatred he felt. It surged through him like a flood, and he expressed it with his 9mm pistol. He spent hours firing at targets as his instructor shouted slurs against the followers of Jesus. But then, when it came time for him to search for a Christian to kill, Budi simply couldn't do it. He and four other boys left.

Budi returned home, but his father's anger drove him away again. He found a job trimming hedges. At night he began reading the Qur'an, which is where he first saw the name Jesus. Intrigued, Budi picked up a Bible and began reading it. One evening alone in his room, he heard a voice say, "I will send a Helper unto you."

Budi couldn't make sense of that sentence until he came across John 14:16: "I will ask the Father, and he will give you another Helper to be with you forever."

At that moment, Budi trusted Jesus as his Savior.

"My whole demeanor has changed," he said, "and God has filled my heart with love. I'm not an angry person anymore. My temper is gone. I don't get mad at people like I did before. Because God loves me, I am able to love others."

Today Budi preaches the gospel in scores of villages and occasionally he meets with the four other boys who left the terrorist training camp. Somehow by the grace of God, all five of them are Christian pastors![17]

The breakdown of law and order is like a deadly wind blowing across our nation and world, chilling the love of many—of most—people. But the fire of God's love keeps us warm and impassioned for Christ as we await His return.

You can make a difference in the World of the End, and you can be the difference in someone's life. It's in so doing that you and I can achieve what the early Christians did—turning the world upside down.

How? By choosing to *be kind*!

*"Hatred stirs up strife, but love covers all sins" (Proverbs 10:12).*

*"Jesus replied: 'Love the Lord your God with all your heart and with all your soul and with all your mind.' This is the first and greatest commandment. And the second is like it: 'Love your neighbor as yourself.' All the Law and the Prophets hang on these two commandments" (Matthew 22:37–40 NIV).*

*"Love your enemies, do good, and lend, hoping for nothing in return; and your reward will be great, and you will be sons of the Most High. For He is kind to the unthankful and evil" (Luke 6:35).*

*"A new commandment I give to you, that you love one another; as I have loved you, that you also love one another. By this all will know that you are My disciples, if you have love for one another" (John 13:34–35).*

*"Let no debt remain outstanding, except the continuing debt to love one another, for whoever loves others has fulfilled the law" (Romans 13:8 NIV).*

*"Love suffers long and is kind. . . . Love never fails" (1 Corinthians 13:4, 8).*

*"Watch, stand fast in the faith, be brave, be strong. Let all that you do be done with love" (1 Corinthians 16:13–14).*

*"As the elect of God, holy and beloved, put on tender mercies, kindness, humility, meekness, longsuffering"* (Colossians 3:12).

*"Since you have purified your souls in obeying the truth through the Spirit in sincere love of the brethren, love one another fervently with a pure heart"* (1 Peter 1:22).

*"Beloved, let us love one another, for love is of God; and everyone who loves is born of God and knows God"* (1 John 4:7).

## Chapter 8

# IN A WORLD OF BAD NEWS,

# *BE THE GOOD NEWS*

*This gospel of the kingdom will be preached
in all the world as a witness to all the
nations, and then the end will come.*

MATTHEW 24:14

In July 1986, thousands of men and women from developing nations boarded airplanes, many for the first time in their lives. They checked into hotels to find something they'd never seen before—indoor plumbing. They were called "barefoot evangelists," men and women with little education or training who hacked through jungles, forded rivers, endured rejection, and took the good news to huts and hamlets in remote nations all over the world.[1]

Evangelist Billy Graham raised millions of dollars to bring eight thousand of these local preachers to the Dutch capital for days of training and encouragement. Never in church history had such a gathering occurred on this scale, with representatives from 180 nations.

In one of his sermons that week, Graham said, "Biblical evangelism preaches Christ alone as the Savior of men. Paul told the Corinthians, 'For Jesus Christ, and Him crucified' (1 Corinthians 2:2). Jesus alone is the way to God. Apart from Him we are spiritually dead and lost. Jesus Christ by His death and resurrection became the Gospel. Jesus Christ is the Gospel!"[2]

Sitting in rapt attention was one particular barefoot evangelist named Joseph, a converted warrior from the Maasai tribe of Central Africa. During the conference, he asked to see Billy Graham. For logistical reasons, very few participants could meet privately with Graham, but Joseph was given a few minutes to tell his story.

As a young man, Joseph heard the gospel on a dusty African road, and he responded instantly by trusting Jesus as his Savior. He soon longed to return to his native village and share the good news of the kingdom of heaven. He went from door to door, telling others what had happened to him. He expected everyone's face to light up. Instead, they were filled with rage.

The men of the village seized Joseph and held him to the ground while the women brutally flogged him with barbed wire. After the beating, he was dragged into the bush and left to die.

Joseph crawled to a watering hole, spent several days recovering, and decided he had either left something out of the story or shared the message incorrectly. He rehearsed his testimony, prayed, and limped back to the village to try again, saying, "Jesus died for you, so that you might have forgiveness and come to know the living God."

He got another flogging.

Recovering a bit, he went back and was whipped a third time, the barbed wire cutting into the old wounds. But this time, one of the women beating him started weeping. As Joseph lapsed into unconsciousness, he saw others beginning to cry. He awoke in his own bed, his former tormenters trying to save his life. As a result of his patient witness, the whole village came to Christ.

Joseph then lifted his shirt to show Dr. Graham the scars marking his chest and back. After he left, the famous evangelist could only say, "I'm not fit to untie his shoes, and he wanted to meet me?"[3]

Have you ever thought of yourself as a barefoot evangelist—someone who can share the gospel anytime, anywhere, whatever your level of training or education, regardless of the reaction? That's what you are! The world is filled with those of us wanting to tell others what Jesus has done for us. And that reality reflects another prophecy fulfilled from Jesus' Olivet Discourse.

Remarkably, on one of the last days of His natural life, Jesus predicted a time when the gospel of the kingdom would be preached to the ends of the earth, heralding the approach of His return. No one in those days could have conceived of it. Jesus of Nazareth was a country preacher in the rural mountains of Galilee. He encountered a lot of skepticism on the rare occasions He came to Jerusalem for the Jewish festivals. He spoke in simple parables and pastoral teachings, and few people outside His circles even knew about Him.

Yet, speaking privately with His disciples shortly before His brutal death, Jesus said that one day His unique message would touch the farthest corners of the globe. It would go to the ends of the earth—and when it did, the world would be near its end.

Of all the prophecies we've studied thus far in Matthew 24, this is the most implausible. One could imagine the continuation of warfare or plagues. Deceivers come and go. But who could imagine that the words of a rural rabbi from Galilee would transform human history, reverberate in every subsequent generation, and be as life-changing two thousand years later as the disciples knew them to be in their own time?

This is our Lord's positive prediction! So far we've looked at a lot of grim prognostications in the Olivet Discourse. But during all those difficult days at the end of history, one thing will be unstoppable: the relentless spread of the gospel of Jesus Christ, in every generation, on every continent, through every difficulty. Like a beam of light through the blackened night, the good news will bring the world its only hope. The message of Jesus—crucified and resurrected—will echo through all the turbulence of time and herald His swift return.

In Matthew 24:14, Jesus said, "This gospel of the kingdom will be preached in all the world as a witness to all the nations, and then the end will come."

## The Unstoppable Message of the Gospel: To the End of the Age

Let's start with the word *gospel*. The Greek term is *evangelion*. You can instantly see how we get the word *evangelism* from it. But look closer. Notice the middle letters: *ev*-angel-*ion*. What is an *angel* doing in the middle of the gospel? Well, the word *angel* literally means "messenger." The Greek prefix *ev*- means "good." So, the word *gospel* literally means "good message" or "good news."

This word appears for the first time in the Bible at the beginning of Jesus' ministry. Matthew 4:23 says, "Jesus went about all Galilee, teaching in their synagogues, preaching the gospel of the kingdom, and healing all kinds of sickness and all kinds of disease among the people."

The gospel is the set of historical facts relating to the life, death, and resurrection of Jesus Christ. It includes the eternal repercussions of these facts for those who place their faith in Christ. They enter a living relationship with God, by grace and through faith. Christ alone offers us forgiveness of sin and eternal life.

Ephesians 1:13 says, "In [Christ] you also trusted, after you heard the word of truth, the [good news] of your salvation."

The word *good* seems like the world's greatest understatement. Our culture loves superlative terms like *amazing, awesome*, and *spectacular*. To us, *good* is far down on that list of adjectives. But the Bible uses *good* as a moral quality of God and a way to describe the nature of the gifts He has given us. In His vocabulary, *good* is far beyond amazing, awesome, and spectacular. It may be His highest adjective. We can pack every superlative we want into those four letters—G-O-O-D—and there will still be an eternity of room left over.

The gospel was sealed and settled by Jesus' shed blood at Calvary and His glorious resurrection. Evangelist D. L. Moody said, "The most solemn truth in the gospel is that the only thing Christ left down here is His blood."[4] When we receive this message by simple faith and confess Christ as Lord of our lives, we become living recipients and embodiments of the good news. In other words, we say yes to Jesus.

Let me tell you about a time when No said yes.

Andrew Lo is the pseudonym for a church planter who works amid danger in a heavily restricted nation. One day Andrew ventured into a village and sought to share the gospel. Only one person listened, and he was wonderfully converted. Ironically, this man's name was No. But No said yes. Eventually his wife and parents also gave their lives to Christ, and now a small church exists in a spiritually dry land—all because Lo shared with No, and No said *yes*.[5]

I can't help but pause here and ask: Have you said yes to Christ? Everything in life and eternity depends on that. Romans 1:16 says, "I am not ashamed of the gospel of Christ, for it is the power of God to salvation for everyone who believes."

Going back to Matthew 24:14, there's something else to notice. The verse says, "This gospel of the kingdom will be preached."

Why is it called the "gospel of the kingdom"? The answer can sound complicated, but I'll keep it simple. The word *kingdom* is short for the "king's domain." Except for once, every time Matthew used the word *gospel*, he couched it in that phrase "gospel of the kingdom."

There's a famous theological phrase that says our Lord's kingdom is "already but not yet." When Jesus came to our world the first time, He planted the kingdom of believers on this planet, infiltrating the nations and placing the foundation for His church. Colossians 1:13 says, "He has delivered us from the power of darkness and conveyed us into the kingdom of the Son of His love." When Christ comes again, He will establish His theocratic kingdom in Israel and reign from there for a thousand years.

So, in one sense, Jesus' kingdom is already here. In another sense, it is still to be established—"already but not yet."

In Mark's version of the Olivet Discourse, Jesus was recorded as simply saying, "And the gospel must first be preached to all the nations" (Mark 13:10). That's the key point. Both the current kingdom of the church age and the coming kingdom of the millennial age spring from the historical facts of Jesus' death and resurrection. The same gospel that makes you and me instant members of God's heavenly kingdom right now will be the power plant allowing Christ to rule the world after His return to earth.

As we study Matthew 24:14 in this chapter, we'll see how this works out as a kind of double fulfillment.

## The Unstoppable Message of the Gospel before the Rapture

The first verses of the Olivet Discourse carry an "already but not yet" flavor. They describe the days leading up to the rapture of the church. Then they rewind and take us through the same general sequence of events during the first half of the tribulation with a deeper level of judgment and distress.

On one level, the Lord Jesus was predicting the deterioration of world events during the epochs leading to His return in the clouds for His people. These are the times we are experiencing now. There will be increasing danger from deceivers, wars, international conflict, famine, pandemics, and natural disasters. Persecution will spike around the world, and love will fade away as a uniting force.

The one positive trend amid these signs is the good news: "This gospel of the kingdom will be preached in all the world as a witness to all the nations, and then the end will come" (Matthew 24:14).

The end of what?

The end of the church age. The presence of the Spirit-indwelled church will be removed from this planet in a flash of time. Graves will become launching pads. Believers will fly into the clouds to be instantly transformed with glorified bodies.

As I said, no one watching the Nazarene that day on Olivet could have imagined this prediction coming true. Yet Jesus repeated His claim in Acts 1:8, telling His disciples, "You shall receive power when the Holy Spirit has come upon you; and you shall be witnesses to Me in Jerusalem, and in all Judea and Samaria, and to the end of the earth."

Shortly after, on the day of Pentecost, three thousand people confessed Christ in Jerusalem and were baptized (Acts 2:41). Many of them went home from the festival of Pentecost, taking the message of Jesus to provinces, cities, towns, and islands throughout the Roman Empire. Soon the number of believers reached five thousand (4:4). The disciples began multiplying exponentially (6:1), and the number of churches multiplied as well (9:31).

From Antioch, the first official church-sent missionaries were commissioned (Barnabas and Paul) and the age of organized missions began (Acts 13). By the early 300s, the Roman Empire had been reshaped by the gospel. Every generation of Christians has spread the news to those around them. Yes, there have been some giants in the list of missionaries and evangelists—Patrick, Wesley, Carey, Moody, Graham. But most of the work has been accomplished by barefoot evangelists—people like you and me who share our testimonies in the same way mariners tell the stories of their rescues from shipwrecks.

Where are we today in world evangelism? The Joshua Project keeps careful track of what God is doing on the earth. According to their research, there are 17,427 people groups on earth, and about 10,000 have been reached with the gospel. There are still 7,414 groups needing the gospel, and many of those are in very restricted nations.[6] That's the bad news.

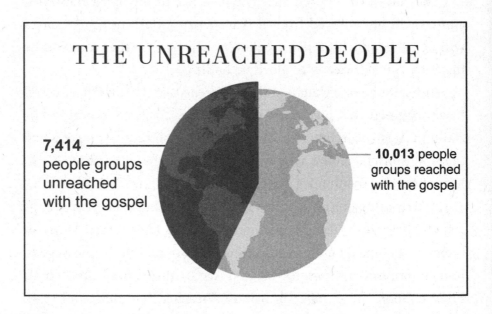

## THE UNREACHED PEOPLE

**7,414** people groups unreached with the gospel

**10,013** people groups reached with the gospel

The good news is that today we're starting to penetrate even the most difficult barriers by means of new technology. The internet is essential, of course. But cheaper methods for setting up satellite TV and radio programs have also allowed preachers to reach directly into the homes of those interested in learning more about Christ—even when those homes are in countries actively hostile to the gospel.

We can see the fulfillment of Jesus' prophecy in real time: the gospel is being preached throughout all the world as a witness to all nations and all peoples. When that process is complete, the stage will be set for the end.

## The Unstoppable Message of the Gospel after the Rapture

As I've said before, the events prophesied in Matthew 24:1–14 will back up and replay after the rapture of the church, this time at a higher volume and with greater intensity. After believers vanish from the earth, there will be a new round of deceivers, including the Man of Lawlessness (the Antichrist), and an unprecedented time of war and rumors of war. Nation will rise against nation and kingdom against kingdom. As we see in the breaking of the seven seals in Revelation 6, there will be famines, pestilences, and earthquakes in various places—all leading up to the middle of the tribulation and to the terrible period known as the great tribulation.

Many people don't realize the first half of the tribulation will be one of the greatest evangelistic awakenings in human history. The gospel will be unstoppable.

You may ask, If the church is removed, who will be evangelizing?

First, I believe the troubles of those days will lead many people to search out the billions of Bibles and New Testaments left behind, along with all kinds of Christian books, recordings, and literature.

Perhaps the greatest distribution of Bibles in history occurred during World War I, with multiple Bible societies printing New Testaments and getting them into the hands of millions of soldiers. One report said, "Soldiers, when they were very badly wounded, had a tendency to produce the New Testament from their breast pocket and read it as they died. This is a phenomenon that was recorded when soldiers who were killed on 1 July 1916—the first day of the Battle of the Somme—were recovered and buried, many of them were found dead with the Bible, or New Testament in their hands."[7]

Could that be a preview of the tribulation?

Second, the Lord is going to commission 144,000 Jewish evangelists who will spread the gospel with the zeal of the apostle Paul to the ends of the earth (Revelation 7:1–4). Everyone converted under their ministries will also reach others, and many of them will be martyred (vv. 9–17). And don't forget the two superevangelists the Lord will place in Jerusalem, described in Revelation 11!

I know you and I are praying for another great awakening to turn around our nation and our world. God has sent massive revivals in the past. Perhaps He will send us one soon. But whether we see global revival or not, we'll be faithful to the cross of Christ until the very end of the age. We can rest assured another great awakening is coming before the ultimate return of Christ—even if it occurs in times of tribulation and even if it happens after the church has vanished.

The gospel of the kingdom will be preached to the whole world, and then will the end come.

## The Unstoppable Messengers of the Gospel: To the Ends of the Earth

The unstoppable message of the gospel will be—and is being—spread by unstoppable messengers. In our generation, that's you and me, taking the gospel to the ends of the earth.

A recent article in *Christianity Today* shared how Christians in the Muslim-majority nation of Azerbaijan are seeing the gospel spread in their land. Emil Panahov, a church planter, grew up in a Muslim family. His father was a Communist. Emil came to Christ at age twelve through the efforts of a local Baptist church, but he became a dancer and was caught up in entertainment. In 2007, Emil tore his meniscus, and doctors told him he would never dance again.

That's when Emil rediscovered Christ and planted a church. He recovered his athletic ability and started using it for evangelistic purposes. During the pandemic, his church baptized sixty-four new believers, a remarkable number for that nation. Restrictions have been relaxed somewhat by the government, and Emil is praying for a massive revival in his home country. Right now, 4 percent of Azerbaijanis are considered Christians. Emil is praying for the day when the other 96 percent will follow Christ![8]

Impossible? Humanly speaking, it would seem so. But Jesus predicted His followers would be unstoppable in taking His gospel to the world. He said, "Behold, I say to you, lift up your eyes and look at the fields, for they are already white for harvest!" (John 4:35). He said, "I will build My church, and the gates of Hades shall not prevail against it" (Matthew 16:18).

When Garrett Kell was a junior at Virginia Tech, he developed an uncanny feeling God was following him. The impression started at a Halloween party he threw in his apartment. He was twenty years old, living with three female roommates, a live-in girlfriend, and a steady supply of weed, cocaine, and alcohol. One of the partygoers was a high school friend named Dave. When Garrett offered him girls and joints, Dave closed the door, looked at him sincerely, and said he didn't do those things anymore. He had become a follower of Christ, and he had attended the party only to ask Garrett to do the same.

Garrett had no intention of accepting Dave's offer, but from that moment he felt haunted. For weeks afterward he was drawn to his Bible like a moth toward a flame.[9]

When spring break came, Garrett's buddy Adam suggested they go to Panama City, Florida. Along the way, Garrett told Adam he felt God was following him everywhere he went. As they neared the beach, a plane flew over their car, pulling a banner that said: "Jesus Loves You—John 3:16."

When they spread their lawn chairs on the sand and cracked open their beer, a small group of students came by, offering them pamphlets and telling them God had a wonderful plan for their lives. That evening while leaving a night club, three vans pulled up, each emblazoned with the words: "God loves you! Believe the gospel! Jesus saves!" It was a team offering free rides to the inebriated spring-breakers.

The next day was rainy, so Garrett and Adam went to a restaurant and wolfed down waffles. Suddenly the doors flew open and about thirty people came in, laughing and talking and carrying Bibles. One of them came up to Garrett and offered to share a Bible study with him.

The next day, Garrett took a walk on the beach and saw a girl sitting by herself. Going up to her, he asked if she'd been in the water. When she said it was too cold, Garrett mentioned he'd have to have a few beers before braving the chill. Looking up at him, she said, "I don't know about that, but God has taught me Jesus is all I need to be happy."

As he returned to the hotel, a lady in a wheelchair motioned for him. Her name was Stacy James, and she asked him what he knew about Jesus.

It sounds like a conspiracy, doesn't it? But Garrett knew the truth. The Lord was following him around, pursuing him like the hound of heaven. Today Garrett Kell is the lead pastor of a church outside Washington, DC. He recently wrote, "Don't underestimate the significance of scattering gospel seed wherever you go. Whether you're on a plane, on a beach, in a Waffle House, driving drunks home, or doing normal life, God is working to call his lost sheep to himself—and he's using you to do it."[10]

How does the Lord use us? What can you do to spread the gospel of the kingdom in these last days? Let me give you three unstoppable ways to share the uncontainable good news.

## In Showing

Our most basic testimony has to do with our lives—daily exhibiting a biblical lifestyle in this ungodly age. That requires a constant walk with the Lord, a desire for personal holiness, a growing attitude of Christlikeness, and a burden to love others and to meet their needs in Christ's name.

Remember Jesus' illustration we explored in the previous chapter: "You are the light of the world. A city that is set on a hill cannot be hidden. Nor do they light a lamp and put it under a basket, but on a lampstand, and it gives light to all who are in the house. Let your light so shine before men, that they may see your good works and glorify your Father in heaven" (Matthew 5:14–16).

Bob Griffin was a legendary missionary pilot—one of the first. While living in Ecuador, he made friends with a military leader named Major Rio Frio. But Bob wasn't able to say much about his faith in Christ. Whenever he tried, the major had a way of holding up his hand to stop the conversation. Nevertheless, Bob continued to exhibit Christ and even flew emergency missions for the major to help stave off starvation among Ecuadorian troops stationed in remote areas.

One day Major Frio told Bob he was being posted to another location. Even though he could take a military aircraft, he asked Bob to fly him to Quito in the small missionary plane. Surprised, Bob agreed to do so.

During the flight, Major Frio turned to Bob and said, "I'd like to know what makes you tick." He went on to explain, "I know you could stay in the US and earn big money flying the airlines or doing some other work. Why do you impoverish yourself to come here to the jungle to help us?"

Over the roar of the engine, Bob took the next fifteen minutes to explain the power of the gospel—that because of what Jesus did for us, we are motivated to share His love with others. He told the major how he had accepted the gift of eternal life through Jesus Christ and then he showed him some Bible verses from the Spanish Bible he always kept in the plane.

Major Frio gripped Bob's arm with both hands and, with tears in his eyes, said, "Mi amigo, that's what I want!" Right there, flying over the snowcapped Andes, Major Rio Frio sincerely prayed, asking Jesus to become his Savior and Lord.[11]

So let me ask: What makes you tick? Does your life so exhibit Jesus Christ that others can see the gospel in you—in your attitudes, activities, demeanor, integrity, and love?

The apostle Peter said two interesting things about this in 1 Peter 3. In verse 1, he told the wives of unsaved husbands to live such a humble and happy life that "if any of [your husbands] do not believe the word, they may be won over without words by [your] behavior" (NIV).

And in verses 15–16, he wrote, "In your hearts revere Christ as Lord. Always be prepared to give an answer to everyone who asks you to give the reason for the hope that you have. But do this with gentleness and respect, keeping a clear conscience, so that those who speak maliciously against your good behavior in Christ may be ashamed of their slander" (NIV).

Live in a way that reflects the power of the gospel, and always be ready to share the message of the gospel when opportunities arise. Those are two simple principles that have eternal impact.

We can apply those principles wherever we are. Eddie Taubensee is a former Major League Baseball catcher who still coaches and instructs players. It gives him an arena to show Christ to players.

"Coaching and my faith go side by side," he said. "Everything about my Christian faith is thinking of others more than myself and serving them and that's exactly what I'm doing as a coach. I'm coming alongside these players doing everything I can to make them the best player they can be and move them on to the next level."[12]

It's really as simple as that. As we look for opportunities and think of others more than ourselves, the Lord lets us come alongside others and influence them.

## In Sharing

At some point in sharing our faith, words are necessary. They can be spoken, printed, or texted, but people need to receive vital information that they often can't find out for themselves. God has revealed it in the Scripture—that He loves us, that our relationship to Him is broken, that Christ has died for our sins and risen from the tomb, and that we need to repent of our sins and trust His good news of salvation.

Sooner or later, we have to communicate these truths to others. That's why the Bible says, "Do the work of an evangelist" (2 Timothy 4:5). Remember that Greek word *evangelion*? The word with an *angel* in the middle of it, meaning "messenger"? The Bible is telling you to be a good news messenger. Every day. All the time.

Doing so doesn't require a theological degree. Just a willingness to share your faith.

Tom Chandler grew up on a pig farm, and his family was very isolated. Before he went to college, he had never been in a grocery store, and he'd only been in a restaurant when traveling with his high school sports team. He was also acutely dyslexic, with a slight speech impediment. And he battled shyness. But he was a great basketball player, and during his senior year in high school he learned he'd been offered a scholarship at LeTourneau University.

Shortly after he arrived on campus, a group of guys invited him to a Youth For Christ meeting. Tom had never attended church— not ever. Before leaving the dorm, the guys formed a circle and said, "Let's pray." Tom had no idea how to pray, and as one guy after another prayed, he became more panicked. When it came his turn, he remembered the Lord's Prayer plaque at his German grandmother's farmhouse, but he couldn't remember the words. So he said, "Our Father, Amen!"

Tom felt humiliated until one of the guys, George, came to his room and apologized for putting him on the spot. George also invited him to attend church with him, and Tom accepted.

Arriving at the church, Tom was horrified when people started singing, "There is a fountain filled with blood drawn from Immanuel's veins." Tom leaned over to George and said, "That's the most terrible thing I've ever heard in my life. How can these people sing about it? They seem to enjoy it."

The pastor was Dr. Kenneth McKinley, a graduate of the school I attended, Dallas Theological Seminary. When he stepped into the pulpit, he opened his Bible and said, "This morning we're going to be in John." Tom only knew the word *John* as a synonym for the toilet, and, perplexed, he leaned over and asked George about it.

George grinned and opened his Bible to the Gospel of John and showed Tom the way. As Dr. McKinley preached, Tom was drawn to his words. Shortly afterward, during a spiritual emphasis week at LeTourneau, a youth evangelist shared the gospel clearly.

"He noted that we're all sinners and Christ died for our sins," Tom recalled. "To become a child of God we need to receive Christ as our

Savior. I found it fascinating and enticing. When he issued an invitation for people to come forward, I responded. I yearned for God's grace in my life. Afterward, the school chaplain met with me. He asked me to quote John 3:16. I didn't know it. He asked me to read it, but I struggled as the words jumbled together on the page."

That didn't stop Tom. He grew in his faith. He went home and shared his faith with his parents, siblings, and elderly grandmother. He was a student at Moody Bible Institute when he learned they all received Christ. Tom and his wife, Clare, became ambassadors for Christ in a range of ministries throughout Asia before Tom's passing in 2020. He was known as the man who went from the pig farm to the ends of the earth—but think of those who spoke into his life![13]

One thing I've learned is that most people don't decide to follow Christ the first time they hear about Him. It takes multiple exposures to the gospel. That's why I don't become discouraged when someone doesn't respond immediately. Sometimes we are seed planters, and someone else will see the harvest. The apostle Paul said, "I planted, Apollos watered, but God gave the increase" (1 Corinthians 3:6).

Philip Schaff, the great church historian, wrote an eight-volume set of books covering the entire sweep of church history. In referring to the growth of the kingdom in the postapostolic era, this is what he said:

> Christianity once established was its own best missionary. It grew naturally from within. It attracted people by its very presence. It was a light shining in darkness and illuminating the darkness. Now while there were no professional missionaries devoting their whole life to this specific work, every congregation was a missionary society, and every Christian believer a missionary, inflamed by the love of Christ to convert his fellow-men. The example had been

set by Jerusalem and Antioch, and by those brethren who, after the martyrdom of Stephen, "were scattered abroad and went about preaching the Word."[14]

That's how the gospel changed the world after the departure of Christ, and that's how the gospel will change the world before He returns. The entire span of Christ's physical absence from this planet—the age of grace from His ascension to His return—has been set aside for the proclamation of the gospel to every generation, to every land, and to every person on earth.

The apostle Peter said,

In the last days scoffers will come, scoffing and following their own evil desires. They will say, "Where is this 'coming' he promised? Ever since our ancestors died, everything goes on as it has since the beginning of creation." But they deliberately forget that long ago by God's word the heavens came into being and the earth was formed out of water and by water. By these waters also the world of that time was deluged and destroyed. By the same word the present heavens and earth are reserved for fire, being kept for the day of judgment and destruction of the ungodly.

But do not forget this one thing, dear friends: With the Lord a day is like a thousand years, and a thousand years are like a day. The Lord is not slow in keeping his promise, as some understand slowness. Instead he is patient with you, not wanting anyone to perish, but everyone to come to repentance (2 Peter 3:3–9 NIV).

In other words, if the Lord is tarrying His return, it's only to give a few more people time to come to repentance. It's only to give you and me enough time to share the gospel with one more person.

Whom can you reach? Ask God to open a door for you to share your faith. Practice your testimony. Learn some verses that summarize the gospel, such as Romans 6:23: "For the wages of sin is death, but the gift of God is eternal life in Christ Jesus our Lord." Cast out fear, and don't be afraid of failure. Trust God to give you the right words at the right time, then leave the results to Him.

## In Supporting

We also share the gospel by sharing our resources for the expansion of the kingdom. When we regularly, prayerfully give our tithes and offerings to our local church and to the other ministries Christ lays on our hearts, He receives our offerings as worship. Then He transmutes them into tangible works of grace. The Philippians provided financial support for Paul's journeys, and his success became their success.

Pastor Chuck Sligh told of a missionary who "returned to England for a brief furlough after many years of faithful service in India. He was invited to a dinner at a great summer resort where he met many women of prominence and position. After dinner he went to his room and penned a letter to his wife. He wrote, 'My Dearest Sweetheart: I've had dinner at the hotel. The company was wonderful. I saw strange things today. Many women were present. There were some who, to my certain knowledge, wore one church, forty cottage organs, twenty libraries and 30,000 Bibles.'"

This man, in his intense longing to "provide the Gospel for spiritually hungering millions in India . . .could not refrain from estimating the silks, satins, and diamonds of the guests at the dinner in terms of his people's needs on the mission field."[15]

That's a good illustration as long as we don't let it "guilt" us into giving. Our silver and gold will perish, but those we win to Christ will join us in heaven forever.

We're living in the last days, and we're the only ones who have good news for this world! The media doesn't. Academia doesn't. The entertainment industry doesn't. The politicians and statesmen certainly don't.

The only place where hope is found is in the proclamation of the good news by the followers of Jesus. And today, people all over the globe are risking their lives to share it.

What a privilege, then, for us to show the gospel, to share it, and to support it.

Perhaps you recall reading about the seventeen missionaries kidnapped recently in Haiti. One of them, Austin Smucker, was there on a short-term assignment. He's a construction worker in Oregon, and he went to Haiti to rebuild homes. As the party drove back from visiting an orphanage, they encountered a roadblock. It was a kidnapping, and the seventeen hostages (including three children) were crammed into a ten-by-twelve-foot room and kept there for two months.

Smucker said the gangsters "would cock the guns in front of us expecting to see us cower in fear. But we didn't because the worst they could do was shoot us and we'd go to heaven."

One night at about 2:30 in the morning, the group snuck out of their prison and embarked on an adventure that reminded some of them of the perilous journey in *The Pilgrim's Progress*. They had to wade through canals, walk around a lake, navigate through a forest of thorns, follow a cow path—and at each junction they circled and prayed for direction. But they all made it to safety.

"I don't have any feelings of anger toward the guards," Smucker said. He also said that it wasn't his first mission trip, and it wouldn't be his last. If anything, he's more than eager to return. "If Satan was attempting to scare me from ever wanting to go on another mission, he was totally unsuccessful."[16]

The message of the gospel is unstoppable—continuing to the end of the age. And the messengers of the gospel are unstoppable—going to the end of the world. That's why I can't stop until the Lord takes me home, and I believe you feel that way too.

People need the Lord. Our world has never needed Him more. Let's all be barefoot evangelists for Christ wherever we go, whatever the cost, until everyone on earth has heard the good news of Jesus and His story, of Jesus and His glory, and of Jesus and His love.

Let's *be the good news!*

*"You are the light of the world. A city that is set on a hill cannot be hidden. . . . Let your light so shine before men, that they may see your good works and glorify your Father in heaven" (Matthew 5:14, 16).*

*"Go therefore and make disciples of all the nations, baptizing them in the name of the Father and of the Son and of the Holy Spirit, teaching them to observe all things that I have commanded you; and lo, I am with you always, even to the end of the age" (Matthew 28:19–20).*

*"Go into all the world and preach the gospel to every creature" (Mark 16:15).*

*"For God so loved the world that He gave His only begotten Son, that whoever believes in Him should not perish but have everlasting life" (John 3:16).*

*"You shall receive power when the Holy Spirit has come upon you; and you shall be witnesses to Me in Jerusalem, and in all Judea and Samaria, and to the end of the earth" (Acts 1:8).*

*"I am not ashamed of the gospel of Christ, for it is the power of God to salvation for everyone who believes, for the Jew first and also for the Greek" (Romans 1:16).*

*"How beautiful are the feet of those who preach the gospel of peace, who bring glad tidings of good things!" (Romans 10:15).*

*"We are God's handiwork, created in Christ Jesus to do good works, which God prepared in advance for us to do" (Ephesians 2:10 NIV).*

*"The gospel is bearing fruit and growing throughout the whole world—just as it has been doing among you since the day you heard it and truly understood God's grace" (Colossians 1:6 NIV).*

*"But sanctify the Lord God in your hearts, and always be ready to give a defense to everyone who asks you a reason for the hope that is in you, with meekness and fear" (1 Peter 3:15).*

Chapter 9

# IN THE WORLD OF THE END,

# *BE DETERMINED*

*He who endures to the end shall be saved.*

MATTHEW 24:13

Flying across the Sahara Desert of North Africa is an incredible experience if you have a window seat. For hours and hours and hours, the only thing you'll see is scorching expanses of sand. The undulating dunes can reach six hundred feet deep. This is the hottest, harshest desert on earth—and it's as big as the United States (including Alaska and Hawaii). Along with sand dunes are gravel-covered plains, salt flats, and barren plateaus.[1]

The eastern boundary of the Sahara is the Red Sea, and the western edge is the Atlantic Ocean. It's like America between the Atlantic and Pacific Oceans—except it's all Death Valley.

One November morning, three men dipped their toes into the

cold waters of the Atlantic in Senegal. Then they began to run. Their goal was the Red Sea, some 4,300 miles away.

Charlie Engle, Ray Zahab, and Kevin Lin were attempting something never before conceived in history: to run across the Sahara Desert. They were doing it to raise awareness of the millions living in Africa without access to clean water. But according to Charlie Engle, he and his friends were also driven to be pioneers. "The challenge of doing something that has never been done before really appealed to us," he said.

Their journey was plagued with challenges, some of which were geographical. Their route ran through six different nations: Senegal, Mauritania, Mali, Niger, Libya, and Egypt. They endured blazing temperatures, sandstorms, government corruption—and sometimes they had to run on two-lane highways where cars whizzed by at more than one hundred miles per hour.

The physical challenges were even greater. The three friends averaged almost forty miles a day, and there were several days in which they ran the equivalent of two marathons back to back—or longer. Each runner had to work through more than fifty blisters on his feet. They lost weight, faced dehydration, and slept no more than five hours each night.

But the biggest obstacle for the runners was mental. "It was much more of a mental exercise than physical," said Engle. "It was much tougher on the mind than it was on the body."[2]

Near the end, the runners were seriously breaking down. Two suffered from severe tendonitis. All three were dealing with intestinal viruses. Their feet had swollen into another shoe size. The youngest runner, Kevin Lin, began to talk openly about giving up and going home. As expedition leader, Charlie Engle encouraged him to stay the course—to keep trying as hard as possible until the last moment.

"It's something I learned from adventure racing," Engle said. "Don't ever pull yourself from the course. Go until you [can't] go because something might change. . . . You keep going."[3]

And they did! They dipped their toes in the cold waters of the Red Sea after 111 grueling days. It was an unequaled feat—or feet!—of endurance.

If you were to check through dictionaries and online resources, you probably couldn't find a better definition for *endurance* than Charlie Engle's statement: *You keep going.*

That's what it means to endure, and that's what Jesus communicated to His disciples on the Mount of Olives.

As we've seen so far, the "signs of the times" about which Jesus prophesied were frightening for many reasons. He warned about deception, both from outside and inside the church. He warned about wars and rumors of wars. He warned about famines and earthquakes and pestilences. He foresaw tribulation and persecution, lawlessness and lovelessness. Even those who professed to be Christians would fall away.

But all the negatives lead to an incredible positive, a phenomenal promise: "But he who endures to the end shall be saved" (Matthew 24:13).

That promise was true for Christ's earliest disciples as they endured attacks from the Roman Empire and the religious leaders of their own community. That promise has been true for all who remained faithful to God's kingdom throughout the ups and downs of history. And that promise is especially critical for believers today as we approach the World of the End.

Yes, we'll certainly face obstacles and difficulties. In so many ways, this world is a giant Sahara Desert. But we have a race to run and we must not give up. We must keep going—with enthusiasm, the strength of Christ within us, and the victory in sight!

# The Strength of Our Stand

Let's look again at the first part of Jesus' promise: "But he who endures."

The Scriptures are packed with admonitions and encouragements for God's people to keep going in tough times. The biblical writers employed many terms to describe this quality of our character: *endurance, steadfastness, faithfulness, perseverance*, and so on. But the basic idea is for followers of Christ to *keep* following Christ all the way, come what may.

Jesus said, "No one, having put his hand to the plow, and looking back, is fit for the kingdom of God" (Luke 9:62).

Paul instructed Timothy to keep going in the face of trials: "You therefore must endure hardship as a good soldier of Jesus Christ" (2 Timothy 2:3). A few verses later, he added, "Remember that Jesus Christ, of the seed of David, was raised from the dead according to my gospel, for which I suffer trouble as an evildoer, even to the point of chains; but the word of God is not chained. *Therefore I endure all things for the sake of the elect*, that they also may obtain the salvation which is in Christ Jesus with eternal glory" (vv. 8–10; emphasis added).

James wrote, "Blessed is the man who endures temptation; for when he has been approved, he will receive the crown of life which the Lord has promised to those who love Him" (1:12).

The Greek word for *endure* in Matthew 24 is *hupomenó*, which is a combination of *hupo* ("under") and *menó* ("stay" or "remain"). So the picture Jesus used to describe those who endure is those who are determined to stay under the load until Christ lifts the load. It refers to submitting to a specific directive or command, choosing to stay in a certain spot even if others have moved on or moved away.

In today's terminology, we might say, "But the person who hangs on to the end shall be saved."

That's not easy! It takes a lot of strength to hang on. We often think of endurance as something passive. Did you ever *endure* a lecture from a boring teacher? What about *suffering through* an all-night shift? In cases like that, we just grin and bear it.

That's not quite what Jesus was talking about.

His call for endurance was a command for His followers to take a stand. To push against the current and refuse to be moved. To hold firm in their convictions and their character even when it seems as if the whole world is against them.

As Paul wrote to the earliest believers,

> Finally, my brethren, be strong in the Lord and in the power of His might. Put on the whole armor of God, that you may be able to stand against the wiles of the devil. For we do not wrestle against flesh and blood, but against principalities, against powers, against the rulers of the darkness of this age, against spiritual hosts of wickedness in the heavenly places. Therefore take up the whole armor of God, that you may be able to withstand in the evil day, and having done all, to stand. (Ephesians 6:10–13)

Pastor Vinod Patil understands that kind of withstanding strength. As a church leader in India, he has witnessed the rise of anticonversion laws passed by the government in recent years—laws specifically designed to increase government-sanctioned attacks against Christian churches.

According to a recent *New York Times* investigation, "Anti-Christian vigilantes are sweeping through villages, storming churches, burning Christian literature, attacking schools and assaulting worshipers. In many cases, the police and members of India's governing party are helping them, government documents and dozens of interviews revealed. In church after church, the very act of worship has become dangerous despite constitutional protections for freedom of religion."

Extremist Hindus have threatened to kill Pastor Patil if they catch him preaching. For that reason, he now lives like a secret agent—zipping through wheat fields and back alleys on his worn-out Honda scooter, making sure he's not followed, praying with families in kitchens and courtyards, and leading secret gatherings in falling-down farmhouses.

"The Constitution gives us the right to preach openly," he told reporters. "Still, you got to be careful."[4] Despite the danger, Pastor Patil has chosen to keep preaching. He has decided to endure. To stand.

Only heaven knows how many Christians are standing *with* him and *like* him on the earth. But we must be among them. "And having done all, to stand" (Ephesians 6:13).

## The Stamina of Our Stand

Running across the Sahara takes *stamina*, which is a word having to do with the resilience of our strength. We not only endure, but we must endure till the end!

Notice the middle section of our Lord's sentence: "But he who endures *to the end* shall be saved" (Matthew 24:13).

The end of what?

That's a widely debated question, and if you read ten commentaries you might get nine different answers. But to me, it's not so difficult.

### Perennial Stamina

First, we're to keep on going until Christ comes for us or calls us home. We are perennials, not annuals. We keep coming back again and again, fruitful, growing, pressing forward with whatever God has for us until, like the Lord Jesus, we can say, "I have glorified You on the earth. I have finished the work which You have given Me to do" (John 17:4).

We're to pursue the Lord's will and calling for our lives until we can say, like Paul, "I have fought the good fight, I have finished the race, I have kept the faith" (2 Timothy 4:7).

We're to wait and watch and work until we can say, like aged Simeon, "Lord, now You are letting Your servant depart in peace, according to Your word; for my eyes have seen Your salvation" (Luke 2:29–30).

We don't do it in our own strength. We pray like the prophet Isaiah: "Be our strength every morning" (Isaiah 33:2 NIV).

And we claim Isaiah's promise: "Those who wait on the LORD shall renew their strength" (Isaiah 40:31).

For those of us living in the World of the End, Jesus' words are a call to keep going as the signs of the times explode around us. We're to run through the smoke, through the trembling earth, through the spinning battlefield, and through the agitation of our age.

We'll never stop until Jesus comes!

This attitude doesn't aways appear as public feats of gallantry. Usually it shows up quietly in our lives. As Dr. V. Raymond Edman of Wheaton College used to tell students, "It's always too soon to quit."

Paul felt the same way. In Acts 20, he told the Ephesian elders, "See, now I go bound in the spirit to Jerusalem, not knowing the things that will happen to me there, except that the Holy Spirit testifies in every city, saying that chains and tribulations await me. But none of these things move me; nor do I count my life dear to myself, so that I may finish my race with joy, and the ministry which I received from the Lord Jesus, to testify to the gospel of the grace of God" (vv. 22–24).

The Living Bible puts it this way: "But life is worth nothing unless

I use it for doing the work assigned me by the Lord Jesus—the work of telling others the Good News about God's mighty kindness and love" (v. 24).

## Personal Stamina

Second, a careful analysis of Matthew 24 gives us a further clue about the stamina we need to endure to the end. It's personal. A fluent student of biblical Greek can tell us that up to this point in the Olivet Discourse, Jesus had been speaking to His disciples in the plural. This isn't obvious in English because our word *you* can be either singular or plural. But the Greek language is different.

Jesus used the plural *you* in the earlier verses:

- "Do you [plural] not see all these things?" (v. 2).
- "Jesus answered and said to them: 'Take heed that no one deceives you [plural]'" (v. 4).
- "You [plural] will hear of wars and rumors of wars. See that you [plural] are not troubled" (v. 6).
- "Then they will deliver you [plural] up to tribulation and kill you [plural], and you [plural] will be hated by all nations for My name's sake" (v. 9).
- "Because lawlessness will abound, the love of many [plural] will grow cold" (v. 12).

But there's a shift in verse 13. The word translated "he" in that verse is the Greek term *ho*, which is singular. "But he [singular] who endures to the end shall be saved." He could have said, "But if you [singular] endure to the end, you [singular] will be saved."

Isn't that interesting? Here in verse 13, Jesus spoke to you as an individual—and to me. He was encouraging each of us to hang on and to keep on hanging on for as long as it takes.

Enduring as a follower of Jesus requires not only strength but also perennial, personal stamina. Don't be afraid to take your stand for what you know is right and what God has communicated through His Word. Then keep standing no matter what comes your way. Let's remain steadfast until the end.

Especially as we approach the World of the End.

## The Satisfaction of Our Stand

Now let's look at the last phrase of Jesus' promise in Matthew 24:13: "But he who endures to the end *shall be saved*" (emphasis added).

Choosing to endure as followers of Christ will require both strength and stamina, but remaining steadfast will ultimately lead to satisfaction.

A biblical word like *salvation* is similar to a diamond, having many facets and faces. That term occurs more than 166 times in the Old and New Testaments, and in different settings it can refer to different things. For example, when the children of Israel were trapped at the Red Sea, Moses told them, "Do not be afraid. Stand still, and see the salvation of the LORD, which He will accomplish for you today" (Exodus 14:13).

In that context, the word implied Israel's deliverance from the pursuing hordes of Egypt. God parted the waters and saved them.

In Romans 13:11, Paul said, "Do this, knowing the time, that now it is high time to awake out of sleep; for now our salvation is nearer than when we first believed." What did he mean by that? He was referring to the moment when we will be saved from this evil world by rapture or resurrection when the Lord appears in the sky.

In Acts 4:12, Peter said, "Nor is there salvation in any other, for there is no other name under heaven given among men by which we must be saved." Here Peter was talking about the eternal salvation of our souls from sin, death, and hell.

What, then, did Jesus mean when He promised that those who endure to the end will be saved?

## What This Salvation Is Not

First, Jesus was not teaching salvation by works. It's not our ability to endure that saves us. It is Christ alone! We can never erase the reality of our sin by our own strength and stamina. We are saved from sin by grace through faith (Ephesians 2:8–9).

Our ability to endure to the end grows out of an intimate connection with Jesus, our Savior. We stand *because* we know Him. We don't earn that connection by standing for Him.

Second, Jesus was not promising us guaranteed safety chutes from every difficulty in life. Indeed, He told us, "In the world you *will have tribulation*; but be of good cheer, I have overcome the world" (John 16:33; emphasis added).

The apostle Paul said, "Yes, and all who desire to live godly in Christ Jesus will suffer persecution" (2 Timothy 3:12).

Peter gave his readers the same warning: "Beloved, do not think it strange concerning the fiery trial which is to try you, as though some strange thing happened to you; but rejoice to the extent that you partake of Christ's sufferings, that when His glory is revealed, you may also be glad with exceeding joy" (1 Peter 4:12–13).

Followers of Jesus will face resistance and encounter trouble and grievous trials and all the more as we move closer to the World of the End.

## What This Salvation Is

What, then, did Jesus mean when He promised that those who endure to the end will be saved? The answer is found as plain as daylight among the final words of the apostle Paul.

In AD 64, the Roman emperor Nero accused Christians of starting the fire that destroyed Rome. In his demonic rage, Nero came against believers with vengeance. As we saw in an earlier chapter, the apostle Paul was tracked down—he may have been betrayed by Alexander the coppersmith—and thrown into the dungeon to await beheading. From there, he wrote his goodbye letter to the church. It was addressed specifically to Timothy, but it was for us all, the final words of the greatest missionary in history, waiting each moment for the soldiers to come and execute him.

Listen to what Paul said at the end of his letter: "The Lord will rescue me from every evil attack and will bring me safely to his heavenly kingdom. To him be glory forever and ever. Amen" (2 Timothy 4:18 NIV).

I believe that's what Jesus meant. That is the satisfaction of our stand. For those who endure to the end, the Lord will rescue them from evil and bring them safely to His heavenly kingdom—and to Him be glory forever and ever!

## The Start of Our Stand

When we consider topics like endurance or perseverance or steadfastness, it's easy to think of them in the abstract or to project them into the future. *When I face opposition out in the future, I'll make sure to endure rather than falter.* Or, *When I'm old and at the end of my life, I'll be sure to remember the importance of finishing strong.*

That's not how it works. The determination to follow Christ regardless of the cost isn't something that just flashes into our souls at the moment of crisis. It starts now and takes a lifetime to develop. It's a day-by-day process.

This is a choice you and I need to make now, at this moment.

There are some practical ways to get started and to sustain our progress, regardless of what's happening to the World of the End.

## Determine to Run Your Race

First comes a God-given, incontestable, undeniable determination to live for Christ whatever the cost. Jesus said, "If anyone desires to come after Me, let him deny himself, and take up his cross daily, and follow Me" (Luke 9:23).

Let me tell you a story from Juyanne James, an English professor and writer, about a man who came to that decision. In her memoir of growing up as an African American woman in rural Louisiana, Professor James described how, once a month, the children's choir was appointed to sing at the church service. People would often stand and share their testimonies.

In James's recollection, one of those testimonies went like this:

I stand before you today to give my testimony. . . . I was young and foolish. I threw away all my money on women and drink. And I heard the Lord calling me over the years, but I wouldn't listen. I didn't slow down for nobody or no thing. Oh, but the Lord, he got such a mighty big hand, and he can reach far and he can reach high and low.

Early one morning, he reached down and grabbed me by my ankles, and I felt like he turned me upside down. He twisted me and turned me until I didn't know which way was up and which way was down. The Devil had got so far up in me that the Lord had to shake him loose. I was driving in my old Ford, but next thing I know the truck had hit this big ol' tree and was rolling this way and that. I knew if it rolled one more time, I wasn't long for this world. I called on Jesus. . . .

And praise the Lord, he heard my cry. I woke up in the hospital some days later, bandages all over me, with a leg near gone. But the first thing I said was "Thank you Jesus. . . ." When I got up from that hospital bed, I decided to follow Jesus.

At that point, said Juyanne James, the whole church erupted in singing, "I have decided to follow Jesus."[5]

You know, that's not a bad testimony. Sometime the Lord grabs our ankles, turns us upside down, this way and that way, until we come to our senses and decide to follow Jesus. Still, we have to say, "No turning back." We have to say, "Though no one join me, still I will follow."

Make up your mind that nothing will deter you from God's will, that no one will draw you from His path, that no foe will defeat you, and that no sin will stop you.

The world behind you, the cross before you!

I mentioned earlier that followers of Christ must be prepared to endure trials of various kinds as we seek to finish that race. Jesus Himself promised we would face tribulation.

But here is a principle and a promise that can help us keep striving: those trials and tribulations can actually become fuel for our endurance. No matter what the world throws our way, we can recycle those experiences in such a way that, through the power of God, our pain is transformed into power.

Don't believe me? Let's see what Scripture says:

- "Count it all joy, my brothers, when you meet trials of various kinds, for you know that the testing of your faith produces steadfastness. And let steadfastness have its full effect, that you may be perfect and complete, lacking in nothing" (James 1:2–4 ESV).

- "Not only that, but we rejoice in our sufferings, knowing that suffering produces endurance, and endurance produces character, and character produces hope, and hope does not put us to shame, because God's love has been poured into our hearts through the Holy Spirit who has been given to us" (Romans 5:3–5 ESV).

Yes, trials and suffering can make it more difficult for us to run the spiritual course set before us—but they don't have to. With God behind us and beside us, suffering becomes steadfastness. Pain becomes perseverance. And trials are transformed into a blessed hope that can carry us even toward perfection and completion, where we lack no good thing.

So, how will you handle the bumps and bruises you receive in your efforts to follow Christ? Will you allow them to slow you down, or will you use them as fuel for your faithfulness? According to Scripture, the choice is yours.

## Determine to React with Radiance

Speaking of choice, it's important that we address our own actions and attitudes when we encounter difficult circumstances. In many ways, how we conduct ourselves throughout our spiritual walk is just as important as how we finish the race.

What do I mean by that? Well, I've known some lemon-faced Christians in my day who were high on endurance but low on love. They were determined to persevere in the midst of persecution, but they made sure everyone around them knew how miserable they were in the process—and they made life miserable for many others who happened to encounter them in the middle of their race.

Such an attitude is not befitting for servants of the King. As Christians, we are called not only to run with endurance and finish the race but to do so in a way that encourages others to follow us. We have been commanded not only to *be* disciples of Jesus but to *make* disciples. And for that to happen, we need to reflect the love and grace and goodness of the One we follow.

My point is this: when we are confronted by all the ugliness Jesus predicted for the World of the End, we can respond by radiating the love of Christ.

We can live, as Paul commanded, "rejoicing in hope, patient in tribulation, continuing steadfastly in prayer" (Romans 12:12).

Remember Peter's commission to the earliest believers, which also applies to us:

> What credit is it if, when you are beaten for your faults, you take it patiently? But when you do good and suffer, if you take it patiently, this is commendable before God. For to this you were called, because Christ also suffered for us, leaving us an example, that you should follow His steps: "Who committed no sin, Nor was deceit found in His mouth"; who, when He was reviled, did not revile in return; when He suffered, He did not threaten, but committed Himself to Him who judges righteously. (1 Peter 2:20–23)

Developing perseverance as a believer in Jesus does not have to be a bitter experience. Yes, each of us will need to endure unpleasant seasons—and this will be especially true as we move closer to the World of the End. But we can use those seasons as opportunities to radiate the love and light of Christ.

## Determine to Reach Your Goal

Being steadfast in your service to God means choosing to run your race, choosing to react to difficult circumstances with the radiance of Christ—and finally, choosing to run until you reach the end of your specific course. It means choosing to keep going until you reach your rest.

I'm reminded of Shinzo Kanakuri, who was the first athlete to represent Japan in the Olympic Games. This was the 1912 Olympics in Stockholm, and Kanakuri was an exciting newcomer for the marathon event. At just twenty years old, he had even set a world record the year before. Expectations were high.

Unfortunately for Kanakuri, things did not go as he planned. After a brutal journey from Japan that took almost three weeks, he was in rough shape prior to the start of the Olympic marathon. To make matters worse, that event was run on an especially balmy day in Sweden with unexpectedly high temperatures and skyrocketing humidity.

About sixteen miles into the race, Kanakuri faltered. He stumbled into a local garden and collapsed. He was eventually found by a Swedish family who nursed him back to health with raspberry juice, cinnamon rolls, and a comfortable bed.

Despite this kindness, the Japanese runner was mortified at his own failure. Uncertain what to do next, Kanakuri quietly returned to Japan to deal with his shame. He left so quietly, in fact, that Swedish officials had no record of what happened to him. He was considered a "missing person" in that country for almost fifty years!

Thankfully, there is a happy ending to Shinzo Kanakuri's story. In 1967, Swedish officials arranged for the now-elderly runner to return to Stockholm and finish the race. Starting where he had left the course all those decades ago, Kanakuri completed the course with a mind-boggling time of 54 years, 8 months, 6 days, 5 hours, 32 minutes, and 20.3 seconds.[6]

Here's my point: despite a decades-long delay, Shinzo Kanakuri completed his race. He reached the finish line at last—and there he was greeted by not only his children but also his grandchildren. Those are grand rewards indeed!

We typically connect the book of Revelation with the chaos and cataclysms we expect to experience at the end of the world—and for good reason. The vision John received on the island of Patmos certainly allows us to peek through the window of time and glimpse many important details about the end of history. As we've seen, those details dovetail perfectly with Jesus' prophetic promises in the Olivet Discourse.

Yet there's a section of Revelation we sometimes forget. In chapters 2 and 3, the Lord Jesus commissioned John to deliver seven letters to the seven churches operating in Asia Minor during his day. Each of those letters carries a specific message that uses imagery and word pictures relevant to those regions. Taken together, they create a wonderful word of encouragement and exhortation from Christ to His church during a season of intense persecution.

There is one specific theme present in each of those letters that is pertinent to this chapter.

See if you can catch that theme based on the verses below:

- For the church at Ephesus: "To him who overcomes I will give to eat from the tree of life, which is in the midst of the Paradise of God" (2:7).
- For the church at Smyrna: "He who overcomes shall not be hurt by the second death" (2:11).
- For the church at Pergamos: "To him who overcomes I will give some of the hidden manna to eat. And I will give him a white stone, and on the stone a new name written which no one knows except him who receives it" (2:17).

- For the church at Thyatira: "And he who overcomes, and keeps My works until the end, to him I will give power over the nations—'He shall rule them with a rod of iron; they shall be dashed to pieces like the potter's vessels'—as I also have received from My Father; and I will give him the morning star" (2:26–28).
- For the church at Sardis: "He who overcomes shall be clothed in white garments, and I will not blot out his name from the Book of Life" (3:5).
- For the church at Philadelphia: "He who overcomes, I will make him a pillar in the temple of My God, and he shall go out no more. I will write on him the name of My God and the name of the city of My God, the New Jerusalem, which comes down out of heaven from My God. And I will write on him My new name" (3:12).
- For the church at Laodicea: "To him who overcomes I will grant to sit with Me on My throne, as I also overcame and sat down with My Father on His throne" (3:21).

Do you see the pattern? In every church, Jesus called the believers to "overcome." To endure. To push past the persecution and the pain they were experiencing. And with every call to "overcome," Jesus included a promised reward.

This is the overwhelming message of Scripture. As children of God, our Savior is calling you and me to be steadfast in taking our stand for His values, His priorities, and His kingdom. He is calling us to remain faithful even when the going gets tough.

Yet He is also encouraging us to receive the rewards He has promised. That starts with eternal life, of course—and if we never received any other gift from our Good Father, we would be blessed beyond all possible comprehension! But He has promised more gifts. He has promised exceedingly, abundantly more than we can ask or imagine (Ephesians 3:20).

I mentioned the following Scripture passages earlier in this book, but they are worth repeating:

- "Blessed is the man who endures temptation," wrote James, "for when he has been approved, he will receive the crown of life which the Lord has promised to those who love Him" (1:12).
- "If we endure," Paul promised, "we shall also reign with Him" (2 Timothy 2:12).

So don't give up in your spiritual walk. Don't allow yourself to be knocked off course or taken out of the race. And if you do stumble, get back up and start running once more. In the words of Sahara-running Charlie Engle, whatever happens, "You keep going." Because your reward is worth it.

John R. W. Stott was one of the greatest Christian leaders of the last century. For many years he served faithfully as rector of All Souls Langham Place in London; he was a peerless preacher, Bible teacher, evangelist, author, speaker, and global leader.

Here is a story Os Guinness told about the final moments of John Stott's race—and how he remained determined to reach his rest as a faithful servant of Christ:

> I knew him over many decades, but I will never forget my last visit to his bedside three weeks before he died. After an unforgettable hour and more of sharing many memories over many years, I asked him how he would like me to pray for him. Lying weakly on his back and barely able to speak, he answered in a hoarse whisper, "Pray that I will be faithful to Jesus until my last breath."[7]

Yes. What a prayer for the end of one man's race, and what a prayer for the World of the End! No matter what we encounter in our world's relentless march toward judgment, let you and me be faithful to our Lord. Let us *be determined*.

# 10 Verses to Help You *Be Determined*

*"Have you not known? Have you not heard? The everlasting God, the LORD, the Creator of the ends of the earth, neither faints nor is weary. His understanding is unsearchable. He gives power to the weak, and to those who have no might He increases strength"* (Isaiah 40:28-29).

*"He who endures to the end will be saved"* (Matthew 10:22).

*"Let us not grow weary while doing good, for in due season we shall reap if we do not lose heart"* (Galatians 6:9).

*"Finally, my brethren, be strong in the LORD and in the power of His might"* (Ephesians 6:10).

*"Take the helmet of salvation, and the sword of the Spirit, which is the word of God; praying always with all prayer and supplication in the Spirit, being watchful to this end with all perseverance and supplication for all the saints"* (Ephesians 6:17–18).

*"We also pray that you will be strengthened with all his glorious power so you will have all the endurance and patience you need"* (Colossians 1:11 NLT).

*"You have need of endurance, so that after you have done the will of God, you may receive the promise"* (Hebrews 10:36).

*"Blessed is the one who perseveres under trial because, having stood the test, that person will receive the crown of life that the LORD has promised to those who love him" (James 1:12 NIV).*

*"Indeed we count them blessed who endure. You have heard of the perseverance of Job and seen the end intended by the Lord— that the LORD is very compassionate and merciful" (James 5:11).*

*"Because you have kept My command to persevere, I also will keep you from the hour of trial which shall come upon the whole world, to test those who dwell on the earth" (Revelation 3:10).*

# Epilogue

We've come a long way in these pages, and I'd like to end with a parable from the nineteenth-century philosopher and theologian Søren Kierkegaard. In his book *Either/Or*, he wrote:

> A fire broke out backstage in a theatre. The clown came out to warn the public; they thought it was a joke and applauded. He repeated it; the acclaim was even greater. I think that's just how the world will come to an end: to general applause from wits who believe it's a joke.[1]

I believe Kierkegaard was correct. In fact, I often feel as if our world is living out his parable in real time. As a culture and as a people, we are increasingly ignorant of what God has said about the end times, and what we face at the conclusion of history. Not only that, but humanity is increasingly hostile toward the idea that an end is coming at all.

As we conclude these final words in *The World of the End*, I don't want to focus on people in general. I don't want to focus on humanity as a whole.

Instead, I want to turn the spotlight directly on you and me.

Make no mistake: everything Jesus warned about in His Olivet

Discourse will happen. Each of His prophecies will be fulfilled, and all His promises will come to pass. We can believe it. We can count on it.

The question is, What we will do about it? What will *you* do about it?

My prayer is that you and I will not sit idly by as the smoke billows through the doors and the flames rise up the walls of our communities. Let us never allow entertainment or comfort or finances or fear or the lust of the flesh or the pride of life or any other earthly thing to get in the way of serving our Savior to the end. To the final moment.

I don't know if we've reached the end of the world. Humanity may have days or decades remaining until the rapture of the church and the grinding, grating *thlipsis* of the tribulation that will follow. As Scripture says, no one knows the day or the hour (Matthew 24:36).

But I do know this: you and I have come to the World of the End. As a planet and a people, we are experiencing the birth pains in preparation for all that God has promised. We are living out the days prophesied by Christ Himself.

Therefore, let us be honest. Let us be calm. Let us be confident. Let us be prepared. Let us be faithful. Let us be kind. Let us be the good news. And let us be determined to live as we should—as children of God who shine like stars in the universe—until the end!

# Index

# Notes

## Introduction
1. Dr. David Osborn, "God and Our Circumstances," PreachingToday. com, May 2005, https://www.preachingtoday.com/illustrations/2005/ may/15921.html.
2. Billy Graham, "10 Quotes from Billy Graham on the End Times," *The Billy Graham Library* (blog), April 8, 2021, https://billygrahamlibrary. org/blog-10-quotes-from-billy-graham-on-end-times/.

## Chapter 1
1. Jeffrey M. McCall, "Cronkite Signed Off 40 Years Ago; It Seems Like an Eon in News Standards," *The Hill,* March 5, 2021, https://thehill. com/opinion/technology/541882-cronkite-signed-off-40-years-ago-it- seems-like-an-eon-in-news-standards/.
2. John MacArthur, *The Second Coming* (Wheaton, IL: Crossway, 1999), 69.
3. Tim LaHaye and Thomas Ice, *Charting the End Times: A Visual Guide to Understanding Bible Prophecy* (Eugene, OR: Harvest House, 2001), 35.
4. John F. Walvoord, "Christ's Olivet Discourse on the End of the Age," Bible.org, January 1, 2008, https://bible.org/ seriespage/1-introduction-2.
5. This paragraph is adapted from *The Jeremiah Study Bible* (Nashville, TN: Worthy, 2018), 1368.

6. Flavius Josephus, *The Wars of the Jews*, 6.267, accessed July 11, 2022, https://lexundria.com/j_bj/6.267/wst.

7. The Babylonian Talmud, Sukkah 51b.

8. Flavius Josephus, *The War of the Jews,* trans. William Whiston, Project Gutenberg, updated August 3, 2013, https://www.gutenberg.org/files/2850/2850-h/2850-h.htm.

9. Josephus, *The War of the Jews.*

10. John MacArthur, *Matthew 24–28: MacArthur New Testament Commentary* (Chicago, IL: Moody Bible Institute, 1989), 15.

11. Walvoord, "Christ's Olivet Discourse," https://bible.org/seriespage/1-introduction-2.

12. Carl G. Johnson, *Prophecy Made Plain* (Chicago: Moody, 1972), 84.

13. James Davis, "Lesson 10: The Study of Future Events," Bible.org, December 4, 2013, https://bible.org/seriespage/lesson-10-study-future-events#_ftnref2.

14. Wayne Grudem, *Systematic Theology: An Introduction to Biblical Doctrine* (Grand Rapids: Zondervan, 1994), 1091.

15. Paul N. Benware, *Understanding End Times Prophecy* (Chicago: Moody, 2006), 15.

16. Jay Yarow, "Here's What Steve Ballmer Thought About the iPhone Five Years Ago," Insider, June 29, 2012, https://www.businessinsider.com/heres-what-steve-ballmer-thought-about-the-iphone-five-years-ago-2012-6.

17. Mark Mitchell, "Ready or Not, Here I Come!" PreachingToday.com, October 2008, https://www.preachingtoday.com/illustrations/2008/october/2102008.html.

## Chapter 2

1. Dan Fisher and Harry Trimborn, "Romania: Death of a Dictator," *Los Angeles Times,* December 26, 1989, https://www.latimes.com/archives/la-xpm-1989-12-26-mn-1001-story.html.

2. Flavius Josephus, *The Antiquities of the Jews,* 20.5.1, trans. William Whiston , Project Gutenberg, updated August 8, 2017, https://www.gutenberg.org/files/2848/2848-h/2848-h.htm#link202HCH0008.

3. Josephus, *Antiquities,* 20.8.6.

4. Sara Toth Stub, "Remembering Hadrian, Destroyer of the Jews," *The Tower,* March 2016, http://www.thetower.org/article/remembering-hadrian-destroyer-of-the-jews/.

5. David Jeremiah, *Until I Come* (Nashville: Thomas Nelson, 1999), 1–2.

6. Dave Breese, *His Infernal Majesty* (Chicago: Moody, 1973), 19.

7. Peyton Shelburne, "Tracking Trust in U.S. Institutions," Morning Consult, May 12, 2022, https://morningconsult.com /tracking-trust-in-institutions/.

8. Sun Tzu, *The Art of War* (Hollywood, FL: Simon and Brown, 2010), 11.

9. Quoted in *750 Engaging Illustrations for Preachers, Teachers, and Writers*, ed. Craig Brian Larson (Grand Rapids, MI: Baker, 1993), 594–95.

10. Michael Guillen, *Believing Is Seeing: A Physicist Explains How Science Shattered His Atheism and Revealed the Necessity of Faith* (Carol Stream, IL: Tyndale, 2021), 22–23, 177–178.

11. Agence France Presse, "Swedish Supreme Court Justice Fined For Shoplifting," *Barron's*, March 31, 2022, https://www.barrons.com /news/swedish-supreme-court-justice-fined-for-shoplifting -01648738207.

12. Os Guinness, *Time for Truth: Living Free in a World of Lies, Hype & Spin* (Grand Rapids: Baker, 2000), 11–12.

13. John MacArthur, *The Truth War: Fighting for Certainty in an Age of Deception* (Nashville: Thomas Nelson, 2007), xi–xii.

14. Guinness, *Time for Truth*, 79-80.

## Chapter 3

1. Chris Hedges, "What Every Person Should Know About War," *New York Times*, July 6, 2003, https://www.nytimes.com/2003/07/06/books /chapters/what-every-person-should-know-about-war.html.

2. C. S. Lewis, *The Joyful Christian* (New York: Touchstone, 1996), 214.

3. John Stuart Mill, "The Contest in America," *Fraser's*, February 1862.

4. Margaret MacMillan, *War: How Conflict Shaped Us* (New York: Random House, 2020), 25–26.

5. Winston Churchill, "Their Finest Hour," (speech, House of Commons, June 18, 1940), International Churchill Society, https:// winstonchurchill.org/resources/speeches/1940-the-finest-hour /their-finest-hour/.

6. Winston Churchill, "We Shall Fight on the Beaches," (speech, House of Commons, June 4, 1940), International Churchill Society, https:// winstonchurchill.org/resources/speeches/1940-the-finest-hour /we-shall-fight-on-the-beaches/.

7. Quoted in MacMillan, *War*, xi.
8. MacMillan, *War*, 5.
9. George Gutchess, *The Great Tribulation: An Exposition of Matthew 24* (self-published, Westbow Press, 2014), comments on Matthew 24:6.
10. Dr. Arnold G. Fruchtenbaum, *The Footsteps of the Messiah* (San Antonio, TX: Ariel Press, 1982), 626.
11. "Ignoring Putin's Threats, US Boosts Support for Ukraine," France 24, January 5, 2022, https://www.france24.com/en/live-news/20220501 -ignoring-putin-s-threats-us-boosts-support-for-ukraine.
12. Evan Osnos, quoted in Rush Doshi, *The Long Game: China's Grand Strategy to Displace American Order* (New York: Oxford University Press, 2021), 2.
13. Doshi, *The Long Game,* 6.
14. "Nuclear Weapons Worldwide," Union of Concerned Scientists, accessed May 16, 2022, https://www.ucsusa.org/nuclear-weapons /worldwide.
15. "Nuclear Weapons Worldwide," Union of Concerned Scientists.
16. M. R. DeHaan, *The Great Society* (Radio Bible Class, 1965), 7–8.
17. Erik Tryggestad, "Ukrainians Count the Days as They Pray," *Christian Chronicle*, May 13, 2022, https://christianchronicle.org/ukrainians -count-the-days-as-they-pray/.
18. This account is adapted from Jayson Casper, "Reaching Youth for Christ During Sudan's Coup," *Christianity Today*, November 3, 2021, https://www.christianitytoday.com/news/2021/november/sudan-coup -christians-youth-for-christ-lebanon-yfc.html.
19. Paul David Tripp, *New Morning Mercies* (Wheaton, IL: Crossway, 2020), Kindle edition.
20. David T. Zabecki, ed., *World War in Europe: An Encyclopedia* (New York: Routledge, 2015), 658. See also Lynne Olson, *Citizens of London* (New York: Random House, 2010), 46–47.

## Chapter 4

1. Michael Poland, "2,773 Earthquakes Were Recorded in the Yellowstone National Park Area in 2021, Annual Report Says," *Idaho Capital Sun*, May 3, 2022, https://idahocapitalsun.com/2022/05/03 /2773-earthquakes-were-recorded-in-the-yellowstone-national-park -area-in-2021-annual-report-says/.

2. Brad Plumer, "What Would Happen If the Yellowstone Supervolcano Actually Erupted?" Vox, updated December 15, 2014, https://www.vox.com/2014/9/5/6108169/yellowstone-supervolcano-eruption.
3. Plumer, "What Would Happen If," Vox.
4. "Volcano Comparisons," Old Faithful Virtual Visitor Center, accessed June 27, 2022, https://www.nps.gov/features/yell/ofvec/exhibits/eruption/volcanoes/compare.htm.
5. Alex de Waal, "Armed Conflict and the Challenge of Hunger: Is an End in Sight?" Global Hunger Index, October 2015, https://www.globalhungerindex.org/issues-in-focus/2015.html.
6. Matt Murphy, "Ukraine Invasion Could Cause Global Food Crisis, UN Warns," BBC News, May 19, 2022, https://www.bbc.com/news/world-europe-61503049.
7. "Hunger Is Spreading Outward from Ukraine," UN World Food Program USA, https://www.wfpusa.org/.
8. "Food Insecurity", City Harvest, accessed June 27, 2022, https://www.cityharvest.org/food-insecurity/.
9. John Ferrari, "America's Shame: About 14 Percent of Military Families Are Food Insecure," *The Hill*, June 19, 2022, https://thehill.com/opinion/national-security/3524996-americas-shame-about-14-percent-of-military-families-are-food-insecure/.
10. Robert Griffiths, "With Food Prices Climbing, the U.N. Is Warning of Crippling Global Shortages," NPR, May 23, 2022, https://www.npr.org/2022/05/23/1100592132/united-nations-food-shortages.
11. Fid Backhouse, "plague of Justinian," accessed July 18, 2022, https://www.britannica.com/event/plague-of-Justinian/additional-info#history.
12. Keith Carlson, "Pandemics in History," *Nursing CE*, June 16, 2020, https://www.nursingce.com/blog/pandemics-in-history/.
13. Nicholas LePan, "Visualizing the History of Pandemics," *Visual Capitalist*, March 14, 2020, https://www.visualcapitalist.com/history-of-pandemics-deadliest/.
14. Fazel Rahman Faizi, "At Least 1,000 Dead in Afghanistan Earthquake," PBSNewsHour, June 22, 2022, https://www.pbs.org/newshour/world/at-least-1000-dead-in-afghanistan-earthquake.
15. Kathryn Schulz, "The Really Big One," New Yorker, July 13, 2015,https://www.newyorker.com/magazine/2015/07/20/the-really-big-one.

16. Schulz, "The Really Big One," New Yorker.
17. Anna Kay Scott, *An Autobiography of Anna Kay Scott* (published by the author in Chicago, 1917), 34–35.
18. Bethany DuVal, "A Hurricane Destroyed Her Neighborhood—and Led Her to Christ," *TEAM Christian Missions Blog*, October 2021, https://team.org/blog/hurricane-led-her-to-christ.
19. Jade Scipioni, "Life Lessons from a 102-Year-Old Who Survived Covid, the Spanish Flu and Two Types of Cancer," CNBC, August 11, 2020, https://www.cnbc.com/2020/08/11/lessons-from-102-year-old-who-survived-covid-flu-pandemic-cancer.html.
20. D. A. Carson, *Basics for Believers: An Exposition of Philippians* (Grand Rapids: Baker, 1996), 93.
21. Pastor Eric Foley, "Ukraine: Church Leaders and His 19 Children Bake One Ton of Bread, Share Gospel in War Zone," Do the Word, April 5, 2022, https://dotheword.org/2022/04/05/ukraine-church-leader-and-his-19-children-bake-one-ton-of-bread-share-gospel-in-war-zone/.
22. Sharyn Alfonsi, "'The Only Big Fear I Have Is Not Succeeding': Legally Blind 15 Year Old Jacob Smith Shredding Expectations in Freeride Skiing," CBS News, March 6, 2022, https://www.cbsnews.com/news/jacob-smith-blind-freeride-skiing-60-minutes-2022-03-06/.

## Chapter 5

1. Andrew Brunson with Craig Borlase, *God's Hostage: A True Story of Persecution, Imprisonment, and Perseverance* (Grand Rapids: Baker, 2019), 93.
2. Brunson and Borlase, *God's Hostage*, 105.
3. Brunson and Borlase, *God's Hostage*, 79.
4. Brunson and Borlase, *God's Hostage*, 244.
5. "'Hostility Toward People Who Embrace Jesus Christ': Pastor Brunson Predicts Intensified Persecution of US Christians," *CBN News*, December 10, 2020, https://www1.cbn.com/cbnnews/us/2020/december/hostility-toward-people-who-embrace-jesus-christ-pastor-brunson-predicts-intensified-persecution-of-us-christians.
6. Bruce L. Shelley, *Church History in Plain Language* (Waco, TX: Word, 1982), 56.

7. Dr. Todd M. Johnson, "Christian Martyrdom: Who? Why? How?" Gordon Conwell Theological Seminary, December 18, 2019, https://www.gordonconwell.edu/blog/christian-martyrdom-who-why-how/.

8. John L. Allen Jr., *The Global War on Christians* (New York: Crown, 2013), 1.

9. "Discover the 50 Places Where Faith in Jesus Costs the Most," Open Doors, accessed May 11, 2022, https://www.opendoorsusa.org/christian-persecution/world-watch-list/.

10. Anugrah Kumar, "China Shuts Down Popular Christian Website Amid Crackdown on Religious Groups," *Christian Post*, April 30, 2022, https://www.christianpost.com/news/china-shuts-down-popular-christian-website.html.

11. Kumar, "China Shuts Down Popular Christian Website," *Christian Post*.

12. *Morning Star News* Nigeria Correspondent, "Herdsmen and Others Kill 18 Christians in Northern Nigeria," Christian Headlines, May 2, 2022, https://www.christianheadlines.com/blog/herdsmen-and-others-kill-18-christians-in-northern-nigeria.html.

13. *Morning Star News* East Africa Correspondent, "Head of Islamic School Burned, Fired for Becoming Christian," Christian Headlines, April 18, 2022, https://www.christianheadlines.com/blog/head-of-islamic-school-burned-fired-for-becoming-christian.html.

14. "Hmong Christian Family Loses Citizenship Rights Due to Faith," International Christian Concern, June 24, 2022, https://www.persecution.org/2022/06/24/hmong-christian-family-loses-citizenship-rights-due-faith/.

15. "Indian Pastor Tortured in Police Custody," International Christian Concern, April 25, 2022, https://www.persecution.org/2022/04/25/indian-pastor-tortured-police-custody/.

16. Sarah Mae Saliong, "Gang Attacks Church-Run Center in Maduro's Venezuela, Hurts and Forces Four Christians to Eat Bible," *Christianity Daily*, March 4, 2021, http://www.christianitydaily.com/articles/11037/20210304/gang-attacks-church-in-maduro-s-venezuela-hurts-and-forces-four-christians-to-eat-bible.htm.

17. Carl and Marsha Mueller, "Remarks by Carl and Marsha Mueller," Permanent Observer Mission of the Holy See to the United States, April 28, 2016, https://holyseemission.org/contents//events/5723cc24e92a84.35067264.php.

18. Jim Denison, "ISIS Martyr Kayla Mueller's Amazing Faith," Christian Headlines, August 26, 2016, https://www.christianheadlines.com /columnists/denison-forum/isis-martyr-kayla-mueller-s-amazing -faith.html.

19. Mueller, "Remarks by Carl and Marsha Mueller."

20. Michael A. Fletcher, "How an Unknown High School Football Coach Landed in the Center of a Supreme Court Religious Liberty Case," ESPN, April 25, 2022, https://www.espn.com/espn/story/_/id/33783970 /how-unknown-high-school-football-coach-landed-center-supreme -court-religious-liberty-case.

21. Todd Nettleton, *When Faith Is Forbidden* (Chicago: Moody, 2021), 116–117.

22. Walter A. Elwell and Philip W. Comfort, eds. *Tyndale Bible Dictionary* (Wheaton, IL: Tyndale House, 2001), 336.

23. R. Kent Hughes, *Acts: The Church Afire* (Wheaton, IL: Crossway, 1996), 216.

24. John Foxe and Harold J. Chadwick, *The New Foxe's Book of Martyrs* (Gainesville, FL: Bridge-Logos, 2001), 348.

25. DC Talk and The Voice of the Martyrs, *Jesus Freaks* (Bloomington, MN: Bethany House, 2020), 54–56.

26. Brunson and Borlase, *God's Hostage*, 208–209.

## Chapter 6

1. History.com editors, "Robert Hanssen, FBI Agent Turned Russian Spy, Is Sentenced to Life in Prison," History, May 9, 2022, https://www .history.com/this-day-in-history/robert-hanssen-fbi-russian-spy -sentenced.

2. Elizabeth Nix, "Robert Hanssen: American Traitor," History, updated April 10, 2019, https://www.history.com/news/robert-hanssen -american-traitor.

3. Louis J. Freeh, "Veteran FBI Agent Arrested and Charged with Espionage," FBI.gov, February 21, 2001, https://archives.fbi.gov /archives/news/pressrel/press-releases/veteran-fbi-agent-arrested -and-charged-with-espionage.

4. Les Parrott, *High-Maintenance Relationships* (Wheaton, IL: Tyndale House, 1996), 95.

5. Phil Waldrep, *Beyond Betrayal: Overcome Past Hurts and Begin to Trust Again* (Eugene, OR: Harvest House, 2020), 16.

6. Abigail Van Buren, "Dear Abby: I Cut Out My Parents After Their Betrayal, but Now They Want to Reconnect," *Chicago Sun Times*, April 24, 2022, https://chicago.suntimes.com/2022/4/24/23038914 /dear-abby-i-cut-out-my-parents-after-their-betrayal-but-now-they -want-to-reconnect.

7. Gordon Fee, *1 & 2 Timothy, Titus* (Grand Rapids: Baker, 1988), 4–5, 296.

8. Richard Wurmbrand, *Tortured for Christ* (Bartlesville, OK: Living Sacrifice Book Company, 1967), 33.

9. Wurmbrand, *Tortured for Christ*, 36.

10. "John Wycliffe," *Christian History,* Issue 3, 1983, https://www .christianitytoday.com/history/people/moversandshakers/john -wycliffe.html.

11. Anne Lim, "During a Dark Time, Ashley Turned to Christ—Now He Wants to Shine His Light," Eternity News, June 2, 2022, https://www .eternitynews.com.au/australia/during-a-dark-time-ashley-turned-to -christ-now-he-wants-to-shine-his-light/.

12. Chloe Taylor, "Step Aside LinkedIn Influencers: This 100-year-old Man Has Been in the Same Job for 84 Years and Reveals His Secret to Longevity," *Fortune*, May 6, 2022, https://fortune.com/2022/05/06 /walter-orthmann-breaks-guinness-world-record-longest-tenure-at -single-company-reneauxview/.

13. Abraham Lincoln, *Collected Works of Abraham Lincoln*, vol. 5, https:// quod.lib.umich.edu/l/lincoln/lincoln5/1:643?rgn=div1;view=fulltext.

14. Quoted in Haddon Robinson, "A Prescription for the Spiritually Challenged," *Preaching Today*, accessed July 7, 2022, https://www. preachingtoday.com/sermons/sermons/2011/january /prescriptionspiritchalngd.html.

15. "Dale Rhoton: 'God Is Able to Triumph,'" Voice of the Martyrs: VOM Radio, https://soundcloud.com/the-voice-of-the-martyrs /dale-rhoton-god-is-able-to-triumph

16. Ben Johnson, "Greyfriars Bobby," Historic UK, accessed June 6, 2022, https://www.historic-uk.com/HistoryUK/HistoryofScotland /Greyfriars-Bobby/.

## Chapter 7

1. Joe Parkinson, Ana Sasani, and Drew Hinshaw, "Afghanistan's Falling Man: The 17-Year-Old Soccer Star Who Plunged From a U.S. Military Jet," *Wall Street Journal,* August 24, 2021, https://www.wsj.com /articles/afghanistans-falling-man-the-17-year-old-soccer-star -who-plunged-from-a-u-s-military-jet-11629834591; Kathy Gannon, "After Afghans fell from plane, families live with horror," *Associated Press*, September 21, 2021, https://apnews.com/article/soccer-sports -afghanistan-middle-east-kabul-58a4e0a9c6343ab78a1985df31e2d729.

2. Dietrich Bonhoeffer, *Life Together* (London: SCM Press, 2015), 93.

3. Frederick Dale Bruner, *Matthew: A Commentary—Volume 2: The Churchbook: Matthew 13–28* (Grand Rapids: William B. Eerdmans, 2004), Kindle edition.

4. Julia Marnin, "Neuroscience Professor Removed from APA Discussion After Saying There Are Only Two Sexes," *Newsweek*, May 14, 2021, https://www.newsweek.com/neuroscience-professor-removed-apa -discussion-after-saying-there-are-only-two-genders-1591697.

5. Ryan Foley, "DOJ Slammed for Likening Concerned Parents to Domestic Terrorists," *Christian Post*, October 6, 2021, https://www .christianpost.com/news/doj-slammed-for-likening-concerned -parents-to-domestic-terrorists.html.

6. "Officials Responded to 37 Fires in Kenosha on 2nd Night of Protests, 1 'Nearly Leveled Several City Blocks'," Fox6 Milwaukee, August 25, 2020, https://www.fox6now.com/news/officials-responded-to -37-fires-in-kenosha-on-2nd-night-of-protests-1-nearly-leveled -several-city-blocks.

7. Dakin Andone, Steve Almasy, and Curt Devine, "What We Know About the Highland Park Shooting Suspect," CNN, July 6, 2022, https://www.cnn.com/2022/07/05/us/robert-e-crimo-highland-park -suspect/index.html.

8. "Loneliness in America: How the Pandemic Has Deepened an Epidemic of Loneliness and What We Can Do About It," Making Caring Common Project, Harvard University, February 2021, https:// mcc.gse.harvard.edu/reports/loneliness-in-america.

9. "'Diseases of Despair' Have Soared Over the Past Decade in US," *BMJ*, September 11, 2020, https://www.bmj.com/company/newsroom /diseases-of-despair-have-soared-over-past-decade-in-us/.

10. James Bryan Smith, *Rich Mullins: A Devotional Biography* (Nashville: B&H, 2000), 25.
11. Smith, *Rich Mullins*, 65.
12. Smith, *Rich Mullins*, 65.
13. Smith, *Rich Mullins*, 67.
14. Michael J. Mantel, "We Can All Help Right Now: Three Simple Ways to Serve With Impact," *Christianity Today*, April 22, 2022, https://www.christianitytoday.com/better-samaritan/2022/april/we-all-can-help-right-now-three-simple-ways-to-serve-with-i.html.
15. Bailey LeFever, "Florida Woman's Pandemic Journey Takes Her from Dishwasher to Political Activist," *Tampa Bay Times*, May 28, 2021, https://www.tampabay.com/news/health/2021/05/28/florida-womans-pandemic-journey-takes-her-from-dishwasher-to-political-activist/.
16. Allison Klein, "Lost Wallet Returned, with Something Extra Inside," *Washington Post*, November 27, 2018, https://www.washingtonpost.com/lifestyle/2018/11/27/lost-wallet-returned-with-something-extra-inside/.
17. Shiloh Lane, "Terrorist Trainee Finds Christ," Baptist Press, September 8, 2011, https://www.baptistpress.com/resource-library/news/terrorist-trainee-finds-christ/. For security reasons, the name was changed.

## Chapter 8

1. "Billy Graham and the Barefoot Evangelists," *Christianity Today*, July 11, 1986, https://www.christianitytoday.com/ct/1986/july-11/billy-graham-and-barefoot-evangelists.html.
2. "Amsterdam 1986 Banner," The Billy Graham Library, July 7, 2016, https://billygrahamlibrary.org/amsterdam-1986-banner/.
3. Adapted from Michael Card, *Immanuel: Reflections of the Life of Christ* (Nashville: Thomas Nelson, 1990),172–174.
4. J. B. McClure, *Moody's Anecdotes and Illustrations* (London: Wakefield, 1887), 47.
5. Brenda Kiš, "When No Said 'Yes'," *ASAP Ministries*, accessed June 22, 2022, https://www.asapministries.org/stories/when-no-said-yes.
6. "Global Statistics," Joshua Project, accessed June 22, 2022, https://joshuaproject.net/people_groups/statistics.

7. "BBC Report Highlights Importance of Bible to WWI Soldiers," Bible Society, May 25, 2021, https://www.biblesociety.org.uk/latest/news/bbc-report-highlights-importance-of-bible-to-wwl-soldiers/.

8. Jayson Casper, "Azerbaijan's Churches Explain Their Evangelism," *Christianity Today*, April 1, 2022, https://www.christianitytoday.com/news/2022/april/azerbaijan-churches-evangelicals-orthodox-evangelism-conver.html.

9. Garrett Kell, "The Stand That Saved My Soul," *All Things for Good* (blog), October 31, 2013, http://garrettkell.com/the-stand-that-saved-my-soul/.

10. Garrett Kell, "When God Chased Me," The Gospel Coalition, April 20, 2016, https://www.thegospelcoalition.org/article/when-god-chased-me/.

11. Bob Griffin, *Cleared for Takeoff* (Traverse City, MI: Harvest Day Books, 2007), 99–100.

12. Danielle Hendrix, "Former Winter Garden Squeeze Coach Heads to Minor League," *Orange Observer*, October 19, 2016, https://www.orangeobserver.com/article/former-winter-garden-squeeze-coach-heads-to-minor-leagues.

13. Adapted from Thomas Chandler Jr., *From Farm Boy to Global Ambassador* (self-published); Tom Chandler, "From Farm Boy to Global Ambassador," *Grace Baptist Church* (blog), November 15, 2017, https://english.gracebaptistchurch.sg/blog/post/from-farm-boy-to-global-ambassador; Caleb Yap, "Passing of Thomas 'Tom' Chandler," *Grace Baptist Church* (blog), January 24, 2020, https://english.gracebaptistchurch.sg/blog/post/passing-of-thomas--tom--chandler.

14. Philip Schaff, *History of the Christian Church, Vol. 2: Ante-Nicene Christianity* (Grand Rapids: Eerdmans, 1910), 20.

15. Chuck Sligh, "Why I Want to Have a Big Part in Missions," Sermon Central, February 26, 2012, https://www.sermoncentral.com/sermons/why-i-want-to-have-a-big-part-in-missions-chuck-sligh-sermon-on-missions-164924?page=2&wc=800.

16. Pat Kruis, "Madras Missionary, Held Hostage in Haiti, Tells His Story," *Portland Tribune*, January 5, 2022, https://www.koin.com/news/madras-missionary-held-hostage-in-haiti-tells-his-story/.

## Chapter 9

1. There are larger cold deserts in Antarctica and the Arctic, but these aren't considered deserts in popular usage. See Rachel Ross, "The Sahara: Earth's Largest Hot Desert," February 24, 2022, LiveScience, https://www.livescience.com/23140-sahara-desert.html.

2. Graham Bensinger, "Run Through Sahara More Than Personal Challenge," ESPN, April 6, 2007, https://www.espn.com/olympics/news/story?id=2828299.

3. Lisa Jhung, "He Ran the Sahara," *Runner's World*, May 8, 2009, https://www.runnersworld.com/runners-stories/a20800083/charlie-engle-of-running-the-sahara/.

4. Jeffrey Gettleman and Suhasini Raj, "Arrests, Beatings and Secret Prayers: Inside the Persecution of India's Christians," *New York Times*, December 22, 2021, https://www.nytimes.com/2021/12/22/world/asia/india-christians-attacked.html.

5. Juyanne James, *Table Scraps: And Other Essays* (Eugene, OR: Resource Publications, 2019), 64–65.

6. Rick Maese, "Lost and Found: How Japan's 'Father of the Marathon' Vanished Midrace," *Washington Post*, August 6, 2021, https://www.washingtonpost.com/sports/olympics/2021/08/06/shinzo-kanakuri-1912-olympic-marathon-stockholm/.

7. Os Guinness, *Impossible People: Christian Courage and the Struggle for the Soul of Civilization* (Downers Grove, IL: InterVarsity, 2016), 34.

## Epilogue

1. Søren Kierkegaard, *Either/Or* (New York: Penguin House, 1992), 49.

# Acknowledgments

With every writing project throughout my writing career, I have worked with incredible people who have come alongside me to help accomplish my goal for each book. That has certainly been true for *The World of the End.*

The journey started, as it often has, with conversations with my wife, Donna. She listens to my ideas and encourages me to follow my instincts. Donna and I have been doing life and ministry together for fifty nine years. My greatest blessing!

Beau Sager is the next most important player on the team. He has been my research assistant for thirteen years and writing books would not be possible without his able assistance.

Rob Morgan and Sam O'Neal also worked with us on this project. They are two of the best read, most servant-hearted men that I know, and I am so thankful for their friendship and assistance.

Damon Reiss, our publisher, was such a positive encourager on many days when I was certain we would not be able to finish the manuscript on time.

Sealy Yates, my literary agent for many years, has provided his usual encouragement and expertise.

Diane Sutherland and Beth Anne Hewett manage my ministry office.

My oldest son, David Michael, became the president of our media ministry this year and led us in the greatest year of growth in our forty-year history and that included record distribution of our books.

Paul Joiner continues to find new and more creative ways to promote our titles, and this year we set new records on YouTube and other social media platforms.

I am totally honored and blessed by all of these amazing people. Thanks to all of you!

# About the Author

**DR. DAVID JEREMIAH** is the founder of Turning Point, an international ministry committed to providing Christians with sound Bible teaching through radio and television, the internet, live events, and resource materials and books. He is the author of more than fifty books, including *Where Do We Go from Here?*, *Forward*, *David Jeremiah Morning and Evening Devotions*, and *The Book of Signs*.

Dr. Jeremiah serves as the senior pastor of Shadow Mountain Community Church in El Cajon, California. He and his wife, Donna, have four grown children and twelve grandchildren.

*stay connected to the teaching of*
# DR. DAVID JEREMIAH

· · · · · · · ·

Publishing | Radio | Television | Online

# FURTHER YOUR STUDY OF THIS BOOK

• • • • • • • • •

## *The World of the End* Resource Materials

To enhance your study on this important topic, we recommend the correlating audio message album, study guide, and DVD messages from *The World of the End* series.

### Audio Message Album

The material found in this book originated from messages presented by Dr. Jeremiah at Shadow Mountain Community Church where he serves as senior pastor. These nine messages are conveniently packaged in an accessible audio album.

### Study Guide

This 144-page study guide correlates with the messages from *The World of the End* series by Dr. Jeremiah. Each lesson provides an outline, an overview, and group and personal application questions.

### DVD Message Presentations

Watch Dr. Jeremiah deliver *The World of the End* original messages in this special DVD collection.

To order these products, call us at 1-800-947-1993 or visit us online at www.DavidJeremiah.org.

# FURTHER YOUR STUDY OF GOD'S WORD

· · · · · · · ·

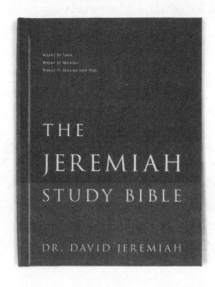

# THE JEREMIAH STUDY BIBLE

**WHAT THE BIBLE SAYS.**
**WHAT IT MEANS.**
**WHAT IT MEANS FOR YOU.**

## MORE THAN 500,000 PEOPLE
## ARE USING **THE JEREMIAH STUDY BIBLE**

*The Jeremiah Study Bible* is comprehensive, yet easy to understand. More than forty years in the making, it is deeply personal and designed to transform your life. No matter your place or time in history, Scripture always speaks to the important issues of life. Hear God speak to you through studying His Word in *The Jeremiah Study Bible*.

## NOW AVAILABLE IN:

- New Kings James Version • Large Print NKJV or NIV
- New International Version • English Standard Version

# STAY CONNECTED TO DAVID JEREMIAH

• • • • • • • •

Take advantage of three great ways to let Dr. David Jeremiah
give you spiritual direction every day!

## *Turning Points* Magazine and Devotional

Receive Dr. Jeremiah's magazine,
*Turning Points*, each month:
- Thematic study focus
- 52 pages of life-changing reading
- Relevant articles
- Daily devotional readings and more!

**Request *Turning Points* magazine today!**
(800) 947-1993 | DavidJeremiah.org/Magazine

## Daily Turning Point E-Devotional

Receive a daily e-devotion from Dr. Jeremiah
that will strengthen your walk with God and
encourage you to live the authentic Christian life.

**Sign up for your free e-devotional today!**
www.DavidJeremiah.org/Devo

## Turning Point Mobile App

Access Dr. Jeremiah's video teachings,
audio sermons, and more . . . whenever and
wherever you are!

**Download your free app today!**
www.DavidJeremiah.org/App

# Books Written by David Jeremiah

• • • • • • • •

- Escape the Coming Night
- Count It All Joy
- The Handwriting on the Wall
- Invasion of Other Gods
- Angels—Who They Are and How They Help…What the Bible Reveals
- The Joy of Encouragement
- Prayer—The Great Adventure
- Overcoming Loneliness
- God in You
- Until Christ Returns
- Stories of Hope
- Slaying the Giants in Your Life
- My Heart's Desire
- Sanctuary
- The Things That Matter
- The Prayer Matrix
- 31 Days to Happiness— Searching for Heaven on Earth
- When Your World Falls Apart
- Turning Points
- Discover Paradise
- Captured by Grace
- Grace Givers
- Why the Nativity?
- Signs of Life
- Life-Changing Moments with God
- Hopeful Parenting
- 1 Minute a Day—Instant Inspiration for the Busy Life
- Grandparenting—Faith That Survives Generations
- In the Words of David Jeremiah
- What in the World Is Going On?

- The Sovereign and the Suffering
- The 12 Ways of Christmas
- What to Do When You Don't Know What to Do
- Living with Confidence in a Chaotic World
- The Coming Economic Armageddon
- Pathways, Your Daily Walk with God
- What the Bible Says About Love, Marriage, and Sex
- I Never Thought I'd See the Day
- Journey, Your Daily Adventure with God
- The Unchanging Word of God
- God Loves You: He Always Has— He Always Will
- Discovery, Experiencing God's Word Day by Day
- What Are You Afraid Of?
- Destination, Your Journey with God
- Answers to Questions About Heaven
- Answers to Questions About Spiritual Warfare
- Answers to Questions About Adversity
- Answers to Questions About Prophecy
- Quest—Seeking God Daily
- The Upward Call
- Ten Questions Christians are Asking
- Understanding the 66 Books of the Bible
- A.D.—The Revolution That Changed the World
- Agents of the Apocalypse
- Agents of Babylon

- Reset—Ten Steps to Spiritual Renewal
- People Are Asking … Is This the End?
- Hope for Today
- Hope—An Anchor for Life
- 30 Days of Prayer
- Revealing the Mysteries of Heaven
- Greater Purpose
- The God You May Not Know
- Overcomer: 8 Ways to Live a Life of Unstoppable Strength, Unmovable Faith, and Unbelievable Power
- In Moments Like These
- The Book of Signs—31 Undeniable Prophecies of the Apocalypse
- Everything You Need: 8 Essential Steps to a Life of Confidence in the Promises of God
- Daily in His Presence
- Answers to Questions About Living in the Last Days
- The Jesus You May Not Know
- Shelter in God
- Forward: Discovering God's Presence and Purpose in Your Tomorrow
- Strength for Today
- Answers to Questions About the Bible
- God Has Not Forgotten You
- Where Do We Go From Here?
- Every Day With Jesus
- After the Rapture
- Living the 66 Books of the Bible
- Answers to Questions About Prayer
- Christ Above All

To order these books, call us at 1-800-947-1993 or visit us online at www.DavidJeremiah.org.